Tria Signs & Wonders

By

Sheila Wheeler

Copyright

Copyright © 2012 by Sheila Wheeler. All rights reserved.
Cover Photograph Copyright © 2009 by Martyn Wheeler. All rights reserved.

Scripture taken from the Holy Bible, NEW INTERNATIONAL VERSION®. Copyright © 1973, 1978, 1984, 2011 by Biblica, Inc. All rights reserved worldwide. Used by permission.

Scripture taken from The Message. Copyright © 1993, 1994, 1995, 1996, 2000, 2001, 2002. Used by permission of NavPress Publishing Group.

ISBN: 978-1-291-08569-3

Second Edition 2013

Thanks go to…

My husband Martyn for his help and support

My son-in-law, John for all his assistance in publishing this book

Mary Parker for editing the manuscript

Stephen Gaukroger and David Coffey for their advice and encouragement

For my family and all the people who have been involved in my story

To God for all His love and care throughout my life

Contents

Introduction	7
Chapter 1 – In the Beginning	9
Chapter 2 – Martyn	13
Chapter 3 – Difficult Times	19
Chapter 4 – The Holy Spirit	25
Chapter 5 – Changed Lives	29
Chapter 6 – With God Nothing is Impossible	33
Chapter 7 - Miracles	37
Chapter 8 – Extra-ordinary Prayer Meetings	43
Chapter 9 – Spring Harvest	49
Chapter 10 – God's Protection	55
Chapter 11 – Friends for a Season	59
Chapter 12 – Trials	65
Chapter 13 – Strange Happenings	71
Chapter 14 – Holidays	75
Chapter 15 – Paul	81
Chapter 16 – Claire	89
Chapter 17 – Moving On	95
Chapter 18 - The Journey Continues	99
Chapter 19 – Walking with God	105

Introduction

Having read the following verses many times, I decided to write down the miraculous things God has done in my life and the things He has shown me along the way. I wanted my grandchildren, Nathan, Amy and Holly, together with their descendants, to understand that God still does incredible things today and to encourage them to expect their own miracles.

Deuteronomy 7:19 – *'You saw with your own eyes the great trials, the miraculous signs and wonders, the mighty hand and outstretched arm, with which the Lord your God brought you out.'*

Deuteronomy 11:2 – *'Remember today that your children were not the ones who saw and experienced the discipline of the Lord your God; His majesty, His mighty hand, His outstretched arm;'*

Deuteronomy 11:5 – *'It was not your children who saw what He did for you in the desert until you arrived at this place.'*

Deuteronomy 11:18 – *'Fix these words of mine in your hearts and minds;'*

Deuteronomy 11:19 – *'Teach them to your children, talking about them when you sit at home and when you walk along the road, when you lie down and when you get up.'*

Deuteronomy 11:20 – *'Write them down on the door-frames of your houses and on your gates, so that your days and the days of your children may be many in the land that the Lord swore to give your forefathers,'*

Deuteronomy 10:20 – *'Fear the Lord your God and serve Him. Hold fast to Him and take your oaths in His name.'*

Deuteronomy 10:21 – *'He is your praise; He is your God, who performed for you these great and awesome wonders you saw with your own eyes.'*

Psalm 40:5 – *'Many, O Lord my God are the wonders you have done. The things you planned for us no-one can recount to you; were I to speak and tell of them they would be too many to declare.'*

Psalm 139:13-16 – *'For you created my inmost being; you knit me together in my mother's womb. I praise you because I am fearfully and wonderfully made; your works are wonderful, I know that full well. My frame was not hidden from you when I was made in the secret place. When I was woven together in the depths of the earth, your eyes saw my unformed body. All the days ordained for me were written in your book before one of them came to be.'*

Chapter 1 – In the Beginning

My story begins in 1945 when my father had a very serious motorbike accident. He was thirty-two years old and a Lance Corporal in the Royal Air Force. Prior to being posted to the Far East, he was given a weekend's leave. Whilst on his way home, he was overtaking a car, and a vehicle travelling in the opposite direction caught his handlebars. This caused him to lose control and swerve off the road into a ditch. In those days, it was not compulsory to wear crash helmets but fortunately he was wearing his leather flying cap, which did give a certain amount of protection. After many hours of lying unconscious, he was found by a local farmer, who took him on his horse-drawn cart to the nearest Hospital - which just happened to be a Maternity Hospital! He had severe head injuries, his neck was broken, along with most of the bones in his body, and he was having epileptic fits.

Amazingly, the bike was not damaged and the dozen eggs which were in the saddle-bags of his bike remained unbroken! The little Hospital had never experienced a patient with such injuries, but my father's auntie, who was a trained Nurse, rushed to his bedside and insisted on nursing him until he recovered. He was unconscious for many weeks, and in fact did not leave the Hospital for over three months and was invalided out of the RAF nine months later. He was left with eighty per cent scarring on his brain, severe epileptic fits and a changed personality. My mother had two small girls under the age of four years old and the doctors gave her the choice - of having my father looked after in a mental Hospital, or caring for him at home. She said she had promised in her wedding vows to stay together through sickness and in health and this encouraged her to make the decision to care for her husband herself.

He did seem to improve, but some years later when she found out she was pregnant, she felt that she could not cope with a sick husband and a third child. She did everything she could to get rid of the baby, even resorting to using a knitting needle! However, God obviously wanted this child to live, and on my mother's birthday October 1st 1948 I, Sheila Diane Wheatley, came into the world.

Many years later, my mother told me about her feelings and how desperate she had been. It seemed that through my birth, my father felt that he had proved to himself he was a 'real man' again. From that time on he began to get much better, although he still had severe epileptic fits and a very quick temper. As I grew up, I was aware that I was loved and wanted by both my parents, and later I was able to share my experience with others who felt that their parents had not wanted them. Over the years this had affected their lives and caused them tremendous hurt and pain. I was able to tell them that, despite whether my parents had wanted me or not, I had a deep awareness that God loved me and there was a purpose for my life and a reason for me to be here - and they too could have that same assurance.

Growing up during the 1950's was very different from today. There were no supermarkets, fast food restaurants or shopping malls. We had no garden centres or recycling centres! The milk, vegetables and coal were delivered by horse and cart and once a month the 'rag and bone man' would also come round with his horse and cart and take away any scrap metal or unwanted items - not many people threw things away in those days! There were fewer cars on the roads (only two or three million!) and there were no motorways! People either walked or travelled by bike or bus, and for longer journeys many would use the coach or steam train! Although my father had owned a car since the early 1930's, we were brought up to walk everywhere and the car was only used for special occasions and really long journeys!

We had few electrical gadgets - no microwave, washing machine, food-mixer, shower or central heating - indeed sometimes in the winter it was so cold that there was ice on the inside of the windows! A refrigerator, telephone and television were all luxuries - although for the Queen's Coronation in 1953 many did rent the very small black and white televisions that had recently been invented! There was great respect for anyone in authority, especially policemen, teachers and even parents! England was classed as a Christian country and Christianity was the only faith taught in the schools.

My sisters and I grew up with a strict Victorian home life, where children were seen and not heard! My father was particularly harsh on my two sisters, but as I was six years younger, he had mellowed a little by the time I came along. He had tremendous mood swings and we children were frightened of him, hating the shouting and rows he often had with my mother and us. He did, however, have a great capacity to love, and I soon discovered that if I showed him love then he would respond kindly.

At the time, our upbringing seemed normal, but strict. When I received bad reports from school (i.e. I had been fighting with the boys! - or not concentrating in class) not only was I in trouble at school, but I was given a thrashing by my father. I received thrashings quite frequently for my school reports! One particular time, when I was a teenager, the wind blew the garage door out of my hands and smashed a pane of glass. My father lost his temper and kicked me extremely hard, leaving my leg very badly bruised. Nowadays, the treatment we received would have amounted to child abuse, but my mother always pleaded with us to make allowances because of my father's brain injury, and told us that he could not help getting so angry. She definitely held the family together and we were devoted to her.

My parents attended Church every Sunday evening. You might wonder how my father related some of his treatment to us with the Bible or his Christian values. He was brought up with strict Victorian discipline and believed in the saying 'spare the rod and spoil the child'. He knew his Bible very well, but he was not so good at putting it into practise in everyday life. I remember watching him kneel by his bed each morning to say his prayers, but if I disturbed him during this quiet time I would be in big trouble! We were brought up to say our prayers, but my early prayers were very much what I call 'God bless Mummy, Daddy and the cat' prayers, or 'shopping list' prayers, where I always seemed to be asking God for things, or to bless people!

Sundays were busy, with us children going to Sunday School in the morning, and a Bible Class called Crusaders in the afternoon. My sisters went to Church with our parents in the evening and I was left on my own at home in bed. I hated those times, and was quite sure that there were burglars in the house! The house seemed to creek and make noises and I would often talk out loud to make it sound as though there was someone with me. In fact, years later I was informed that an intruder had got into the house whilst they were all at Church, but unknowingly I must have frightened him away!

Back to Crusaders - now renamed Urban Saints - a Christian Interdenominational Youth and Children's Organisation, which has been established since 1906. Each Sunday, we received points for attending and remembering the memory verse, our badge and Bible. When we had attended fifty consecutive Sundays, we were given a special Bible with the Crusader badge engraved on it. This was considered a great achievement, and I still have mine, which was given to me in 1959. My sisters and I have always valued the teaching and grounding of the Scriptures we received through going to Crusaders.

I cannot remember a time when I did not believe that Jesus loved me and died on the cross to take away my sins, and that one day I would be with Him in Heaven for ever. I had a lot of head knowledge about the Bible but lacked a deep relationship with Jesus Christ. At sixteen I was baptised, sang in the choir, taught in the Sunday School, and knew exactly what I believed.

However, it was not until some years later, I found out that there was so much more God wanted to reveal to me.

Chapter 2 – Martyn

I met Martyn Wheeler at a Baptist Missionary Society Summer School. It was a Christian holiday, for young people who came from different Churches all over the UK and they would stay in boarding schools for a week or two during the summer holidays. Martyn was not a Christian, but was part of the youth group from a Baptist Church in Wakefield, Yorkshire. To be a member of their group, you had to attend Church once on a Sunday, and this he duly did, although he wasn't particularly interested in God.

I was sixteen and was a voluntary helper at the summer school, which meant I helped with light household duties, washed up, served meals etc. and in return was given a free holiday. The voluntary helpers sat at the head of each table at mealtimes to serve the young people, who were encouraged to circulate to different tables. However, this group of young men from Wakefield insisted on sitting at my table for every meal! On the last day at breakfast, as I finished my cornflakes, I realised there was some writing in indelible ink on my plate -'we love Sheila' - I kept that plate for many years!

After the holiday, a few of the group wrote to me, but only one young man persisted in writing - nineteen year old Martyn. We met again the following year, when his youth group went to Summer School at Seaford, Sussex. It wasn't too far from Worthing where I lived, and a friend gave me a lift in his car. By this time, I was nursing at Worthing General Hospital and did not have much free time.

My parents decided that a good career for me would be with the police or as a nurse. However, as I wasn't quite tall enough to be a police woman, I chose to be a nurse. They also felt that there were various attributes that qualified me, in their eyes, for the noble profession of nursing! I had looked after my grandparents for a year when I was thirteen, as their health was not good. My parents had bought a house in Worthing and my grandparents lived in it. I went to help them with shopping, collecting prescriptions, and housework until my parents sold our house in Harrow. I was quite happy to be there as I attended a new school and spent much of my spare time at the local stables. I had been 'horse mad' since I was eight years old and had saved up all my birthday and Christmas money to buy my first pony for fifty pounds! I used to do a lot of show jumping and taught riding in order to help pay for my horse's keep.

Sadly, my grandmother died of angina and a year later, when I was fifteen, I came home from school and found my grandfather dead. My mother always said that he died of a broken heart because he missed his wife so much. Growing up, I had often helped Mum with my father when he suffered his more severe epileptic fits - so they felt that I would make a good nurse! My greatest desire would have been to work with horses, but that was not considered a 'proper' job for a young lady!

Martyn and I were teenagers during the so-called 'swinging sixties'. We did not realise what an impact this decade would have on the world - so much seemed to change. Teenagers were given more freedom and were not prepared to come under authority as they had done in previous generations. Music changed radically with the era of the Beatles, The Rolling Stones, Cliff Richard etc. We listened, on our little transistor radios, to the Pirate Radio Ships which were anchored off the coast of England. They played all sorts of popular music that the BBC was not transmitting, until eventually the Government closed them down and Radio 1 was born! Fashion changed dramatically with the appearance of the mini-skirts, hot-pants and bikinis, and for the men – flared trousers, flowery shirts and ties, long hair and platform shoes. Our generation was introduced to drink, drugs and sex in a way that had not existed before among the young. Society and its values were becoming very different.

Martyn invited me for a week's holiday to stay with him and his parents in Wakefield, and that was when I knew our friendship was going to last! Unfortunately, when my father realised that we were not just 'good friends,' he was not happy. As far as he was concerned, Martyn was not the right person for his daughter. He was not a Christian, his parents lived in a Council house, and all his family supported the Labour Party - definitely the wrong politics! Martyn was a clerk, with no prospects and no money. Everything was against him - and worse, as far as my father was concerned, he came from the North of England (anywhere north of Watford Gap was the North for him!) Due to my father's brain damage, and my birth, he was particularly possessive of me and I do not think anyone would have been good enough to marry his daughter!

Looking back, I can see that our family backgrounds were very different, but of course that doesn't matter when you are in love, and it certainly would not matter so much in today's society. There was a big divide between the working class and the middle class people - 'the have's' and the 'have not's'. Martyn's Dad had been invalided out of the Army and was Head Gardener at Pinderfields

Hospital in Wakefield. He had a couple of extra jobs gardening to bring in enough money so that they could live comfortably. He came from Hilmarton, near Calne in Wiltshire and his father (Martyn's grandfather) was a gardener at the local Vicarage and a Verger and Sexton in the Church. He worked hard to feed his nine children and they lived in a little two-bedroom cottage. The children all slept 'top to tail' in one room and down the garden was an outside toilet with two seats side by side – a large one for the adults and a smaller, lower one for the children! Apparently, if they needed the toilet during the night, as there were no torches, they would light their way by carrying a little candle in a jam jar, which had a piece of string around the top for a handle!

Martyn's maternal grandfather and great-grandfather were born and bred in Alverthorpe, near Wakefield, Yorkshire. They were both coal miners and I remember his grandfather telling me that he had started work at thirteen years old and his first week's salary was equivalent to our thirty-seven pence (seven shillings and six pence in old money!) Martyn's grandparents lived in a Council house which originally had no bathroom, but just had an outside toilet. 'Bath-time' involved them bringing in an old tin bath from the garden, which they put by the fire and filled up with kettles of hot water that had been heated over the fire. Eventually, a bathroom and toilet were fitted upstairs and for the first three years of Martyn's life he and his parents lived with his grandparents. Martyn's grandfather was a Representative for the National Union of Mineworkers, which meant that he was involved in liaising between the workers and the management. He also became Deputy Mayor and he and Martyn's grandmother worked tirelessly for the Labour Party, and for the community.

In contrast, my father's mother came from a very rich family. Her father and his brother owned a large family draper's store called Tompson Brothers, which was situated in the centre of London. My mother often told how she remembered watching ladies, dressed in beautiful long dresses, arrive at the shop in their horse-drawn carriages and they were met at the door by men dressed in frock coats. Apparently, my grandmother ran away to get married because her parents did not approve that she wanted to marry a train driver! There was terrible snobbery from the rich people towards the 'working classes'. As a child, my father was unable to meet very often with his father's mother as she was regarded as being 'lower class'. He had very fond memories of the few times he was allowed to visit her and remembered at the age of twelve being heart-broken when she died. My mother's parents were never really accepted into my father's family, as her Dad was only a printer and her grandfather a butcher! They were classed as 'country folk!'

My mother first met my father at the Young People's Fellowship at College Road Baptist Church, in Harrow. She was captured by his good looks and the fact that he owned his own car and house! His parents had recently sold a hotel in Kingsgate, Kent. They employed live-in servants and owned a large house in Harrow, as well as a house in Ferring, Sussex, which they rented out as a holiday home. They also owned various properties in Cricklewood, London which they rented out. As an only child who was brought up in a fairly modest home, my mother was very much drawn to this rich family! Ironically, despite the family snobbery, most of their money had been passed down from earlier generations, who were licensed victuallers (pub owners!) and coal merchants!

I was not aware of my family background until many years later but, looking back, it now helps me to understand a little of what was to come!

To return to our story - Martyn and I wrote to each other and spoke on the phone most days. There were no mobile phones and as he did not have a phone at home, Martyn used the telephone-box at the end of his road. He spent many cold, wet, and windy evenings talking to me from that phone-box! Anyone who has had a long-distance relationship knows that absence makes the heart grow fonder. However, it was not until my father told me I was to stop phoning and writing to Martyn, that I decided to take drastic action! I went to the Matron of Worthing Hospital and explained about my father's brain damage and possessiveness over me and requested a transfer to Pinderfields General Hospital in Wakefield, Yorkshire. At that time, I was a second-year student training to become a State Registered Nurse, and it was unusual to have a transfer in the middle of one's training. However, I was given a transfer and much against my father's will, I duly went to live in the Nurses' Home in Wakefield.

Due to the shift work, I now rarely attended Church, although occasionally I would go to Wakefield Baptist Church with Martyn. I still prayed and read my Bible, but did not have a close walk with the Lord. The fact that Martyn was not a Christian did not matter to me, as I was quite sure I could change him and he assured me that we would still attend Church when we were married! In the Bible, Christians are advised not to become 'unevenly yoked' with non-Christians for a reason. It can lead to difficulties, sometimes with the couples themselves, or later when they are bringing up their children. Often, it is the Christian who ends up backsliding in his or her attendance of Church and their walk with the Lord.

On September 4th 1968, Martyn's parents held a family party to celebrate their 25th wedding anniversary and we decided to announce our engagement. Martyn had wanted to ask my father's permission to get married when we visited my parents earlier in the year, but my mother begged us not to say anything. That night, we went up to 'our phone-box' and Martyn told my father that we wanted to get engaged. He was not prepared for the explosion. As far as my father was concerned, it could not have been worse if I had been pregnant or marrying a black man. He came from an era when both these would have brought disgrace on the family. He spent most of the phone call telling Martyn what a terrible daughter I was.

After that, sadly we had no contact with my parents for three years, apart from when we sent an invitation asking them to come to our wedding on October 25th 1969. We received a reply saying, 'It is with regret, Mr. and Mrs. Wheatley will not be able to attend their daughter's wedding'.

I must have been a great disappointment to them as, during the year we were engaged, I also left nursing. We knew we could not afford to get married on our existing wages – Martyn's salary was ten pounds per week and after my expenses at the nurse's home had been paid, I was left with four pounds! Having taken a short-hand and typing course at school, I left nursing and went to work at a local Estate Agents. I rented a bedsit, comprising of one small room with basic furniture, and shared a bathroom with four other occupants of the house. We set a target of saving one thousand pounds before we got married; so as food cost money, I barely ate! In fact, on our wedding day I weighed only seven stone. Martyn was fine, as he was living at home with his parents and very well looked after! Unfortunately, due to the problems with my parents, Martyn's mother was not really happy about our getting married. On one occasion, she even suggested that I should leave and go back down south! We certainly did not have an easy time those first couple of years.

In those days, one did not 'come of age' or become an adult until you were twenty-one years old. So we waited until after my 21st birthday and three weeks later we were married in St. John's Church of England Church, Wakefield. Martyn's mother's brother, Uncle Reg, walked me down the aisle on a wet and windy day! We could not afford a honeymoon, but we hired a car and drove to Wiltshire to see some of Martyn's relatives who had not been able to attend the wedding. Our first night of married life was spent in a bed and breakfast guesthouse in the centre of Stow-on-the-Wold. We were kept awake for much of the night by the Church clock, which chimed every half hour throughout the night! Our second night was spent at a farmhouse in Ogbourne St. George, Wiltshire, where we were woken by the cows being milked at 5.00am!

Having had two rather disturbed nights, we decided to return to Wakefield! We rented a first floor flat which had one bedroom, a lounge and kitchen and we shared a bathroom with the elderly couple who owned the house. We did not have much money, yet nothing could spoil our happiness. Our world seemed idyllic. Little did we know what the future had in store for us!

Chapter 3 – Difficult Times

We had no communication with my parents for a couple of years, and I never thought of them during the day, but suddenly I started having terrible nightmares. My father was always chasing after me and invariably trying to strangle me. I woke up from these dreams dripping in sweat and very distressed. We decided to make contact with my parents, so we hired a car and drove from Yorkshire to Sussex to see them. We did not tell them that we were coming, as we thought they might refuse to see us. Twenty miles from their home, my hands were visibly shaking on the steering wheel. We did not know how my father would react, so we decided to see my mother first, where she worked at Gifford House, an Ex-Servicemen's Hospital in Worthing. She was overjoyed to see us, and we both shed a few tears! She suggested we met my father whilst he was on his own at home, so off we went.

When we arrived, he was out walking with the dog, so we sat on the doorstep and waited. As he walked up the drive, his dog, Kim obviously remembered me and greeted me with great excitement, jumping up and licking me, and making up for the cool reception my father gave us! When we told him that we had just driven down from Yorkshire he asked if we would like a cup of tea. I thought I was helping when I took the pint of milk from the fridge and turned it upside down to mix up the cream. (In those days, we used to have bottles of milk that had an inch of cream on the top which, when shaken, would mix into the milk.) However, the bottle had already been started, and as I turned it upside down, the milk came out all over the floor. Imagine my horror - here was I wanting to make a good impression, and only causing what could have been disaster. I think my father must have been in shock that we were even there, and instead of getting cross, he told me not to worry because the dog would lick up the milk!

I do not remember much about our conversation, but I do recall when my mother came home from work she pretended to be surprised that we were there, and when my father asked if we would like to stay for supper, she just happened to have enough fish for four! During the evening, he asked where we were staying and when we told him that we had not booked anywhere, he said we could stay with them. Things were not easy at first. My father wanted to talk about the past and what a terrible daughter I had been. However, I pointed out that we must ignore the past and look to the future, or there was no point in our staying.

God only knows why I had those nightmares, they certainly seemed to be the catalyst that instigated our decision to visit my parents, and afterwards they never returned. I know that if we had not gone home that day, we would have missed out on all the years of happiness which followed. Since then, I have always felt that in family disputes, the younger members need to be the ones who are prepared to 'eat humble pie', as it were. Often the older people are too proud to realise that they might be just as much at fault! Certainly my father would never have made the first move to contact us! That visit was the first of many and over the years our relationship developed and grew. Martyn became a much loved son-in-law, helped by the fact that all the issues which made him so unsuitable in the beginning, as far as my father was concerned, all changed – career, religion, and even politics - but those are stories for later!

The next difficult episode in our lives was when we were told we might not be able to have any children. We had been married for about three years and I had some tests which showed one of my fallopian tubes was blocked. At this point, we were not too concerned. We had bought a three-bedroom bungalow, I was enjoying working in a local Building Society as a shorthand/typist/clerk, and Martyn had just started a career in a Building Society in Leeds. We decided that instead of having children, we would buy a colour television and a Ford Capri - both of which were classed as luxuries in those days! Of course, as soon as we did this, I became pregnant! Obviously, the Capri was not big enough for a baby, so we exchanged it for a Ford Escort (the car that is, not the baby!)

Within days, I had a miscarriage. I was sixteen weeks pregnant, and we were both heart-broken. The events of that night are still very clear in my mind. We had called the Doctor, as I was experiencing some bleeding and a lot of pain. He said that I should go to the hospital and Martyn duly drove me there. By the time we arrived, I was rolling around the car in agony. He ran to get a wheelchair but an off-duty Sister saw us and called a porter to bring a trolley. I was then taken straight to a ward. Up to this point, I had not received any pain relief and was screaming in pain. For those who don't know, at this stage the baby is fully formed and the labour pains are exactly the same as one would experience for a full-term pregnancy. By this time it was the middle of the night and I remember thinking that I must be keeping all the other patients awake! Eventually, the Doctor arrived to give me some pain relief and I felt easier. Feeling as though I needed to go to the toilet, I asked for a bed pan and at that point the baby was born. I remember being afraid to look into the bed pan and just caught a glimpse of its contents. They just took it away and we never knew what happened to it.

Up to that point, we had not really wanted children but now we felt that our one chance of having a child had gone. We were distraught. We received no counselling or help, the Doctors just told us to try again and good-meaning people said that it was nature's way of getting rid of a baby that obviously had something wrong with it. Nowadays, when one has a miscarriage or a child dies in the womb, there are organisations and bereavement Counsellors one can turn to for help and support. Parents are sometimes encouraged to name their dead babies and even have a funeral. Had we been attending Church, I know we would have experienced the love and care from the people there. God certainly seemed very far away from us during those days. However, of course it was us that were far from Him; He was there all the time, just longing for us to turn to Him.

Three months later we were overjoyed to find out that I was pregnant again and in August 1973 Claire Michelle arrived, weighing in at 7lb 2oz. Everything was wonderful - except she never stopped crying! Thinking she must be hungry, I stopped breast-feeding and gave her a bottle. My mother-in-law was quite sure I should use National Dried Milk, which she had given Martyn when he was a baby! Since then, we have found out that this was the worst milk we could have given Claire, as she had colic and the milk caused her even more problems. The only time she stopped crying was when I took her out in the pram. I walked miles, but the minute we returned home and the pram stopped, she would start to cry again. When Martyn came home from work at 6.00pm I could not cope anymore with this screaming baby, and he would take over, walking up and down with her on his shoulder. She had a dummy to pacify her but every time she dropped it out of her mouth, she screamed even louder until it was found. At night, sometimes Martyn would get out of bed at least a dozen times to give the dummy back to her. Fortunately, he was always able to go straight back to sleep again!

By the time she was three months old, I was ready to put my head in the gas oven, or to put my screaming baby on the fast lane of the motorway! Many times, I begged Martyn to stay at home with me because I could not cope, but he was unable to take time off (there was no 'paternity leave' in those days!) His parents did not help me and of course my family were all down south. We had no close friends and we were not going to Church at all. I still prayed, but my prayers did not seem to make a lot of difference!

Eventually I went to the Doctor for help, and was diagnosed with post-natal depression. He prescribed pills and arranged to see me on a weekly basis. He gave me a regular appointment to ensure I had something on which to focus my mind, in order to get me through to the next week. Well-meaning people told me that I should not be depressed because I had a beautiful baby, and this period would soon pass. However, when you are going through depression you cannot pull yourself out of it, even though you want to. The good news was that, as Claire grew and started on solids, the colic eased and she began to move around and was not so frustrated. She was always awake a great deal, but the health visitor encouraged me by saying she would be a very intelligent child because she was so active. That is not particularly helpful when you are longing for your baby to spend more time asleep!

It was not until Claire was about eighteen months old and I was helping in a local playgroup, that I realised I was feeling much better and was able to stop the pills overnight. The Doctor had told me that I would have to be weaned off them slowly, but we went away for a few days and forgot to take them with us!

Unfortunately, about the same time, Claire and I caught German measles and at that point, I realised that I was six weeks pregnant. Following blood tests, the Doctor informed me that I must have a termination, because the baby could be born disabled, deaf, blind or with a hole in the heart. Having not had any teaching from Church regarding termination or abortions, and there was not the publicity surrounding the subject, as there is today, it never occurred to me to question the Doctor's suggestion. So, at eight weeks I went into Hospital to have a termination. Nowadays, my thinking would be very different, but at that time the medical profession was my only guide. We were told if we wanted to have another child, to just try again. A few weeks later I became pregnant, but sadly had another miscarriage.

Looking back over my life, it seems that nearly every experience I have been through, God has enabled me to use it to help others, hence the reason why I wanted to write this book. Certainly, later when I ran a Mothers and Toddlers Club, I shared my personal experiences with the mothers and was able to help many who were having similar problems.

Eventually, after a very difficult pregnancy and birth, Paul Michael was born, weighing in at 6lbs. The doctor decided to perform a ventouse delivery, which involves putting a 'plunger' on the baby's head and sucking the baby out. Unfortunately, he came into the world so quickly that the umbilical cord was caught around his neck, so the first few minutes of his life were quite traumatic. He was shown to me and then placed in an incubator to recover from the birth. I was taken back to the ward and Martyn came in to see me. (In those days fathers were not allowed to be at the birth.) He then went back to work but after a few hours I complained of terrible pains and was rushed back to theatre for an operation. I had a large haematoma (a very large blood blister) which developed underneath my stitches. As I had been given a big dose of pethidine during the birth, followed by an anaesthetic, this caused my blood pressure to drop extremely low, and I nearly died. However, praise God, I lived to tell the tale!

Martyn came back to see me at the evening visiting time and to his surprise was asked to go into the waiting room. He had not been there very long, when he saw a lady being wheeled past on a trolley with, in his words, 'drips and tubes coming out of everywhere'. He remembers thinking 'some poor husband is going to get a shock!' You may have guessed - that lady was me! The hospital had not contacted him about my being taken back to theatre and when he had left me earlier that day I had been fine, so it really was a shock for him.

Both Paul and I recovered fairly quickly but I was warned to be prepared that post-natal depression most likely would return. However, this time things were very different. Paul was a much quieter baby and did not suffer from colic. I was also extremely busy, due to the fact that Martyn had just been appointed Chief Clerk with the Leeds Permanent Building Society in Luton, Bedfordshire. This involved him working in Luton all week and only coming home at weekends. So, I was left with a toddler and a newborn baby and had to pack up everything ready for moving house. I certainly did not have time to be depressed!

God had not featured much in our lives up to this point -although He was obviously looking after us and leading us to where He wanted us to go.

Chapter 4 – The Holy Spirit

When we first arrived in Luton, we decided to have both children dedicated to God. Martyn's mother had been particularly upset that we had not christened Claire. Apparently, she had been informed that if a baby died without being christened, it would be buried in un-consecrated ground. Somehow, she seemed to think that God would not accept a child in Heaven who had not been christened. Martyn's grandfather, whose job it was to dig the ground ready for the coffins, had first-hand experience of seeing children who were not christened being buried outside the walls of the Churchyard. In the Baptist Church, babies are dedicated to God and the parents thank God for them and make promises to bring them up to know about Jesus. When the child is old enough, he or she can then make their own adult decision as to whether they want to become a Christian and be baptised. We were visiting my parents in Sussex, and the Minister at the Church where I had previously been a member, agreed to dedicate both Claire and Paul together.

After this, I felt it important that Claire should attend Sunday School. By now she was four years old and I went with her to Stopsley Baptist Church. She did not want to be left on her own, so they invited me to stay with her. The teachers soon found out that I knew all the songs and actions and invited us to the next Family Service. This time Martyn and Paul went with us and from then on we began to attend regularly. Paul went into the crèche, and Claire attended the Sunday School without any further problems. There was a membership of about forty people and although Martyn wasn't a Christian, he enjoyed going and we made lots of friends.

Over a period of time, I began to feel something within me telling me to start a worship band at the Church (I now realise it was the prompting of the Holy Spirit). On speaking to the Minister, he told me that he and two guys who played guitars were feeling the same. The three of us joined together - Peter, Paul and Sheila - and we led worship on Sunday evenings. The weekly practices were held in our house, and Peter and Paul brought their wives with them. Often more chatting took place than practice, but during that year Martyn was drawn into the Church more and more, due to the fellowship and friendship he received. Eventually, the Minister moved to Liverpool, leaving the Church without a leader for a year, but the membership worked together and actually grew in strength and numbers.

We noticed some people in the Church had something different about their lives - they seemed to radiate the love of Jesus in all they said and did. They talked about Baptism in the Holy Spirit, tongues, miracles, signs and wonders, things we had not heard about before. I was brought up in an era where the Holy Spirit was not talked about in the Baptist Church, and I began to feel like a second-class Christian because I did not have what they had! It actually made me quite cross, as I was sure of what I believed - that healing and miracles all happened in the Bible, but not today!

We were invited to attend an evening at Luton Town Football Ground, where the speaker was Colin Urquhart. He was the Vicar at St. Hugh's, Luton, and the members of the Church were experiencing miracles, particularly in the area of healing. Hundreds of people attended the evening but when he said God wanted to heal people with all sorts of illnesses, I began to feel uncomfortable. He asked anyone to go forward who had trouble with their eyes, ears, heads, backs, stomachs, legs, feet - in fact he hardly left out any part of the body! Many streamed on to the pitch to receive healing. I was so sceptical, and came away even more entrenched in my position - that healing did not happen today.

Some friends invited Martyn and me to a Full Gospel Business Men's Dinner. The FGB is an organisation founded by Demos Shakarian to reach businessmen all over the world with the Gospel of Jesus Christ. People who do not usually attend Church are invited to a local Hotel for dinner and afterwards someone gives a testimony or a talk about Jesus. In this case, after the talk, there was a time of singing. People around us were raising their hands and speaking and singing in strange languages. We had never experienced anything like it. We hated that part of the evening, and thought that the people were very strange!

However, we could not stop thinking and talking about what we had seen and heard. (Does that remind you of Acts chapter 2 in the Bible - the reaction of the people when the disciples first spoke in tongues?) I started to read a book called *They Speak With Other Tongues* by John Sherrill, which is about a sceptical reporter who sets out to prove that speaking in tongues (other languages) does not exist today, however he ends up speaking in tongues himself!

Martyn was becoming more interested in Christianity, continually firing questions at me. We would read our respective books - him trying to find out more about Christianity and me trying to prove that healing and the Baptism of the Holy Spirit and tongues did not happen today! We went to a Cliff Richard Gospel Concert and Cliff shared about his life and why he became a Christian. Martyn began to think, if someone like Cliff Richard could be a Christian, maybe he could too!

One Sunday evening, I stayed at home with the children and Martyn went to Church. When he came home he asked if we could get a babysitter for Friday evening's prayer meeting. I nearly fell off my chair in surprise - that he should want to go to a prayer meeting! Anyway, we went along, and heard people praying and saying sorry for things they had done wrong that week. Martyn suddenly realised that he did not have to be perfect to become a Christian. This had been a real stumbling block for him and it was at this prayer meeting that he gave his life to the Lord, at the age of thirty-four.

Our excitement was tinged with sadness, when we found out that a couple in the Church, with whom we had just made friends, had been asked to leave, due to the fact that they spoke in tongues, raised their arms in worship and said things such as 'Hallelujah' and 'Praise the Lord'. (We were told that you did not do such things in Baptist Churches in those days!) I was upset and invited the lady to have coffee with me, as I felt sure that she needed cheering up! To my surprise, she arrived, not the least bit unhappy. She started sharing about her life and how she and her husband had become Christians. They literally had a Pentecost experience, as in Acts chapter 2, in their bedroom, which had transformed their lives. I questioned this lady about the Baptism of the Holy Spirit, tongues, healing, hearing God's voice - all these things I believed happened in the Bible, but surely not today?

The morning passed so quickly and soon it was time for me to collect Paul from playgroup. Before she left, I asked her to pray for me. She agreed to do this; however, knowing I was sceptical about 'laying on of hands', she did not touch me. As she prayed, I felt a feeling of warmth and joy flood over me. It seemed my mouth was forced open and my tongue began to move involuntarily and I started to speak a few words in a strange language. She asked me, what was my favourite chorus or hymn, all I could think of was the children's chorus - 'My God is so Big' - so we duly sang this in tongues!

I felt incredible as I floated to playgroup. Fortunately, my neighbour, who normally walked with me, was out. I had never been drunk, but I felt drunk! I thought of the words in Acts chapter 2 when, on hearing the Disciples speaking in tongues, the people thought they were drunk. I kept hearing these words in my head 'Be still and know that I am God'. On returning home, I was rushing around in bare feet, preparing Paul's lunch and walked into the leg of his wooden high-chair, ripping one of my toes out to 'ten past two' position. I was in agony! A neighbour took me to hospital where they said it was broken and bound the three toes together. The doctor laughed at me when I told him we were going on holiday to Newquay at the weekend - to a Hotel that had lots of sports facilities. He said that I would not be able to do much 'on that foot' for a while! I returned home and was only able to get around on my bottom but continued to prepare for our family holiday. It occurred to me that, perhaps if I had listened to that 'still small voice' and sat down and thought about what had taken place in the morning, maybe I might not have broken my toe - who knows? I rang my friend to tell her about my toe and she said that she would pray for me.

When we arrived in Newquay, I covered my bandaged foot with a plastic bag so that I could go swimming. However, just moving it in the water was extremely painful. The next morning at breakfast, Martyn said "What shall we do?" I suggested that we try to go for a walk! He laughed, but that morning we walked three miles and during the course of the week, I played squash, went horse-riding, swam and walked miles. My toe was completely healed, although still a little out of shape - it still is, possibly to remind me that God definitely heals today!

As I thought about the whole experience, I realised God had answered all my queries. Tongues and healing do exist today and I did hear God's voice; and something else, I don't know what made me think about this but, until then, I had been terrified of flying. Nothing would make me go in an aeroplane. Suddenly, I realised that I was not frightened anymore. If God Almighty, the Creator of the universe could reach down and touch me of all people, then He would surely take care of me wherever I was. Perhaps, sub-consciously, I had been afraid of dying - now my fear was gone. I knew whether I lived or died, the Lord would take care of me.

Chapter 5 – Changed Lives

Following this experience, my life was transformed. My faith went from head knowledge of knowing the Bible and about Jesus, to having a walking, talking, intimate relationship with Him. I could not stop talking about what had happened. (Back to Acts chapter 2 again!) However, knowing what happened to my friend, I now had a problem. What would happen to me at Church - would I be asked to leave? A new young Minister, Stephen Gaukroger, had just been appointed and we invited him and his wife Janet for a meal, where I told them about my experience. He soon put my mind at rest, when he informed me that he did not have a problem with anyone speaking in tongues, as long as it was all done in order, according to Scripture.

From this time on, I had a fresh resolve to win people for Christ and a boldness to speak about Jesus. Two neighbours, who attended the Church, also had an experience of the Holy Spirit in their lives. One lady phoned the minister at 6.30am to say – "I've found it, I've found it", only to be told – "I'm very pleased. However, I was not aware that anything was lost!" She soon came to realise that the Holy Spirit is not an 'it' but a 'He' - a person, God Himself. Nevertheless, her experience was life-changing for her. On moving to Luton I started a baby-sitting circle amongst the neighbours, and we met once a month for coffee and a chat whilst the children played. The three of us from Church shared our experiences with the Mums, and they were so interested we decided to turn our coffee mornings into a Bible study. Soon some of the Mums started coming to Church; it was a very exciting time.

Even at the school gates God gave me opportunities to share with others. I became friends with a lady called Lyn, who started coming to our Bible Studies. Months later, Martyn and I started a Discipleship course with her and her husband Roger (who admitted later that he came along, not fully appreciating what was happening). During the course, he gave his life to the Lord and they have remained our best friends ever since. Our lives followed very similar journeys, where we experienced problems with jobs, teenagers, and elderly parents. We have shared many happy and sad times. We have laughed, cried and prayed together - but all that started from gossiping the Gospel at the school gate!

Martyn asked our new Minister to baptise him and a date was set for the day of our 12th wedding anniversary, October 25th 1981. The problem we had was, how could we share this with Martyn's parents? They did not go to Church, but we were praying that they would become Christians, so we wanted them to be there. Whilst we were on holiday in Wales with them, we broached the subject. They agreed to come, but felt that, as Martyn had been baptised as a baby into the Church of England Church, there was no need for him to be baptised again. Martyn shared that he wanted to make his own adult decision to let people know that he had decided to follow Jesus, but sadly they did not understand.

The day of the Baptism had been particularly busy. A number of guests had come for lunch and there was a tea at the Church for friends and the Church fellowship. Martyn and I realised that we had been so busy throughout the day that we both felt tired and quite tense. We held on to each other, and there in the Church Hall amongst all the people, we just stood and prayed for God's peace to come upon us. To this day I can still remember the incredible peace that flooded into our lives that afternoon. No longer did we feel tired or stressed – the peace of God replaced all that, and we were able to really enjoy the Service.

The words of Jesus came into our minds from John 14:27 -

'Peace I leave with you; My peace I give you. I do not give to you as the world gives. Do not let your hearts be troubled and do not be afraid.'

Sadly, Martyn's parents found the service quite upsetting, especially when it came to the time for Martyn to be baptised. As he was going under the water, the Minister said that he was saying goodbye to his old sinful life, and as he came up out of the water he was acknowledging he was a new man starting a new life in Christ. Unfortunately, Martyn's mother took it as a personal insult, that he was not happy with his old life and the way she had brought him up. As far as she was concerned, he was perfect in her eyes, so he did not need to improve, and the service had an adverse effect on her, leaving her very cross.

We continued to pray for them, and one day I felt the Lord spoke to me through reading Joel 2:28-29 -

'And afterwards, I will pour out my Spirit on all people. Your sons and daughters will prophesy, your old men will dream dreams, your young men will *see visions. Even on my servants, both men and women, I will pour out my Spirit in those days.'*

That week we went to a Bible Study, and the person leading the evening based it on these verses. This seemed like confirmation and I felt assured that Martyn's parents would one day become Christians.

Years later, I had the privilege of leading Martyn's Dad to the Lord. He was eighty-five and living in a nursing home. After suffering a great deal of pain and illness throughout his life, I said, "Just think if you knew Jesus, one day when you get to Heaven you will have a new body, no more pain, and we will be able to run and jump together".

He replied, "You really believe that don't you? I wish I could believe it too". I suggested that all he had to do was pray with me - acknowledge that Jesus died on the cross to take away his sins - believe that He came alive again and ask Jesus to come into his life. He would then be assured of eternal life, and 'that new body' to go with it! He said that he wanted to pray, so there in his wheelchair, in the garden amongst the lovely flowers, I prayed and we said "Amen" together.

A few days later, I asked him if he remembered our conversation and what we had prayed about. I was overjoyed when he said that he did. I know that one day we will be reunited, and we will run and jump together because of the promise of Joel 2:32 -

'Everyone who calls on the name of the Lord will be saved.'

Chapter 6 – With God Nothing is Impossible

My parents had always attended Baptist Churches but they had received little teaching about the Holy Spirit or healing. In those days, they would talk about the Trinity, but it was never explained that God, Jesus and the Holy Spirit are one – just as the sun is made up of heat, light and power; or water, steam and ice, are all one. I remember a very difficult discussion we had with my father, when Martyn and I tried to convince him that Jesus is God. He spent a long time looking in the Bible for every reference where Jesus is called the Son of God, but we tried to get him to see that Jesus was God in human form.

John 1:1 - *'In the beginning was the Word and the Word was with God and the Word was God'*

and Hebrews 1:3 – *'The Son is the radiance of God's glory and the exact representation of His being.'*

You could not argue with my father, as in his opinion he was always right, so in the end we agreed to disagree. However, we all went together to Church that evening, where the visiting preacher was my cousin's husband and he just happened to preach a sermon on John 1:1-18 - how that Jesus, God, and the Holy Spirit are one!

I felt I should tell my parents about my experience of the Holy Spirit, healing etc., so when we next visited them, I duly related what had happened to me. My story was met with a stony silence and at the first opportunity the subject was changed. I found out later that my father thought I had been dabbling in the occult! It was not mentioned again, until about a year later when he was in Hospital recovering from a hip replacement operation. Martyn and I called to see him soon after the operation and found him to be quite emotional following the anaesthetic. He took my hand and said, "I know I can tell you this. I can't tell anyone else, but I know you will understand - I believe that I have been healed by God, through the hand of the Surgeon". I knew then why I had felt compelled to tell him about my healing a year before. It was for such a time as this.

After 'my experience of the Holy Spirit', Martyn and I read a number of books about people whose lives had been transformed by the power of the Holy Spirit. One such book was called *Arise and Reap* by Isabel Chapman. We were amazed by her faith and the outworking of that in her life. We read about countless miracles of people's lives being changed, incredible healings and how God provided in impossible situations. It was like reading a modern-day book of Acts, and our faith was raised to believe that God could do anything.

About the same time, a neighbour's little baby was taken into hospital with meningitis. The baby had an extremely high temperature and the Doctors gave little hope that he would recover. I remember standing at my kitchen sink, praying in my new-found prayer language. I did not know what I was saying. I only knew that I had run out of English words to say and was desperate for God to heal this little baby. I had never before prayed so intensely from deep within my spirit. A tremendous peace came over me and I was able to go to bed and sleep soundly. Next day, we heard that during the night the baby's temperature had returned to normal and the Doctors were calling the child 'their miracle baby'. When the parents returned home, we shared with them that we had been praying and believed God had healed their baby. Although not Christians they did acknowledge that a miracle had taken place.

Martyn and I led a housegroup which consisted of some Church members and a few people who were not Christians. We met each week and discussed questions about the Bible and the Christian faith. These meetings were held in a home belonging to a couple, where the husband was not a Christian. His wife became pregnant with their third child, but when she had a scan it showed that there were some lights on the baby's kidneys. Apparently, this meant that the kidneys had something wrong with them and could not function properly and the baby would die soon after it was born. The couple were heartbroken and were offered a termination.

We gathered together with some friends from Church to pray about the situation, and each of us had an overwhelming feeling God did not want this pregnancy terminated, and that the baby would live. We shared this with the couple and they decided to continue with the pregnancy. The husband said that if the baby was born healthy, he would acknowledge God had answered our prayers and would become a Christian! The day the baby was born, Martyn and I went to see them in hospital. To our astonishment, as we walked into the ward, the husband was extremely angry. The birth had gone well but the baby still had the lights on the kidneys and was not expected to live very long. We were devastated and could not believe our ears. We had been so sure God was going to heal this baby. However, we continued to pray and seek God's guidance.

Two weeks later, the parents were asked to take the baby to see a Consultant at a London Hospital. As they did not have a car, we offered to take them. We waited anxiously whilst the baby and her mother were sent for scans. The father asked the Consultant how long would the child live? To his amazement, the Doctor replied that he thought that she would be fine! He went on to say that he wanted to scan her two older sisters, because he believed that the problem might be hereditary. This meant that all the females in the family could have these lights on their kidneys. This was confirmed on another visit, when the two sisters and the mother's sister were scanned, and the lights showed up on all their kidneys - yet they were all healthy! How we praised the Lord that this little baby's life had not been terminated. Indeed this must have happened nearly twenty years ago and the last we heard she has grown into a healthy young woman, but sadly her father did not become a Christian.

My sisters asked Martyn and me to join them on a family holiday at the Christian conference centre Lee Abbey, in Lynton, Devon. My oldest sister Valerie is single, and my other sister Christine, or Kitty as she likes to be called, is married to John; they have three children and live in Scotland. It seemed a good opportunity for us all to meet and for the cousins to get to know each other better. Lee Abbey is a large house set in beautiful grounds, amidst woods and fields that seem to literally roll down towards the private beach nestled at the bottom of the hill. It is such a peaceful place and refreshes mind and spirit, however perhaps not the body, after walking up and down the hill to the beach a few times! During the evenings we enjoyed camp fires, services, singing and opportunities to pray with people. We met a German family with the surname 'Blessing' (what a beautiful name for Christians to have) who invited us to stay with them in Stuttgart. Some months later we went to see them and I absolutely loved every minute of the flight. In fact, since then, we have flown to many parts of the world and I praise the Lord that He took away my fear of flying and of dying!

Whilst at Lee Abbey, someone recommended I read a book by Jackie Pullinger called *Chasing the Dragon*. This is about a lady who went to live and work amongst the Triad Gangs in Hong Kong and how, through the power of the Holy Spirit, the drug addicts are wonderfully saved and released from their drug addictions. I found this book so incredible that I could not stop talking about it and encouraging others to read it. Indeed before I reached the last chapter I gave it away to someone else to read!

Some months later, a missionary couple en-route to South Africa, came to stay with us. When the lady heard that I had never read the last chapter, imagine my surprise when she just happened to have a copy of the book in her handbag! She gave it to me, and as I turned to the last chapter, I saw it was entitled 'Walk in the Spirit'. I really felt God wanted me to read this and take it on board and continually walk in the power of His Holy Spirit.

Chapter 7 - Miracles

A few months after we had moved to Luton, Martyn became an area representative for the Building Society. This meant that he was given a Company car, and his job was to obtain investments/business from Solicitors, Accountants, Bank Managers and Estate Agents. Eventually, he became the Manager of the new Dunstable Branch, and part of his job involved dining out most days with the various professional bodies. It is interesting to think that this boy from the Council estate, who had left school at fifteen without any recognised qualifications, was now mixing with professional people, most of whom had attended private schools, Universities, and gained various degrees! It proves that if you work hard, and with God's help, you can achieve your dreams.

Martyn and I were invited to various functions and dinner dances, especially around Christmas time. At one such dinner dance, I remember sitting next to a Solicitor who had drunk too much. Our conversation happened to turn to Church, and I told him that I was a Sunday School teacher. He seemed quite interested, although before long he was sitting under the table with his bottle of port, and I was quite glad to escape his company!

Some years later we met again at a Church function. Although he did not remember me, during our conversation he told me that he had given up drinking and become a Christian. Even more amazing, years later we met his son, David, who told us that when he was born, there was something very wrong with him mentally and physically. By the time he was two years old, he was almost a human vegetable; he could not stand or walk. He sat on the floor all day long with a totally blank expression on his face unable to hear and hardly able to see. Apparently, the amount of brain damage he had left no hope that David would ever improve through medical treatment. However, his mother spoke to two people who were members at St. Hugh's Church, Luton, who started praying for him in their 'healing group'. Immediately, David began to change and within two weeks he was not only standing, but could see, hear, laugh and was beginning to talk and even sing. Twenty years later David was the Drama and Performing Arts Director at Luton Christian Fellowship, and we had the privilege of knowing him during that time. How marvellous that nothing is impossible with God.

In 1982 Martyn became a Building Society Manager for the Leeds in St. Albans and the company insisted that we move nearer the Branch. An Estate Agent told Martyn that he had just the house for him to look at in Harpenden. When we walked in the front door, we knew that this was the house for us. It was a four-bedroom detached house, whereas we were living in a three-bedroom semi. We did not want to move too far from the Church, and we didn't feel we could afford this new house. So we prayed about it, and felt that if God wanted us to move, He would provide the money that we needed. We even came to the point of turning the house down but within days both our respective parents offered to lend us the deposit, so we were able to go ahead and move. The Company did not seem to bother that we were only moving seven miles, and they paid all our moving expenses, carpets, curtains, school uniforms etc. Thank you Lord.

Even in the process of moving house God was changing me. Another 'problem' I encountered was raising my hands during worship. More people were doing this, and even though I felt that I wanted to, something stopped me. Perhaps I was self-conscious, or worried about what others might think! Anyway, when we were selling our house, some Christians came to look round, and we just happened to start talking about raising hands in worship! I remember this lady said, "Just think about it as though a burglar came into your house, pointed a gun at you, and demanded money, valuables etc. Rather than get shot, you would put both your hands up and give him everything. Imagine in worship, that you are saying to Jesus, I surrender all to You, take everything, every part of me, I hold nothing back". From then on, I did not have a problem.

A few weeks after we moved to Harpenden a friend of mine invited me to a local Bible Study group, consisting of ladies who attended different Churches throughout Harpenden. There I met a lady called Jennie. She and her husband Bill had been missionaries in Papua New Guinea and they believed that God had called them back to England. Whilst abroad they had prayed with various people about where they should live and, through someone speaking in tongues and another interpreting, God had given them two counties - Hertfordshire and Bedfordshire. A week before they were due to come home they had nowhere to stay, and they met another missionary couple who shared that they had a house in Harpenden, Hertfordshire, which they offered to missionaries coming home on furlough. That is how Bill and Jennie and their two children came to live in Harpenden!

The following Saturday we invited this little family to tea. Our children were the same ages and had similar interests and soon became firm friends. Also that afternoon we had invited our Minister, Steve to tea (his wife Janet was in America visiting her family). The previous Wednesday evening, at the Church meeting, it had been decided to advertise for an Assistant Minister. So, it was at our house Steve met Bill and some months later Bill became the Assistant Minister and moved into a house near the Church, in Bedfordshire. There was the Hertfordshire/Bedfordshire connection God had given them months before. How great to be part of God's plan!

Meeting Bill and Jennie opened our eyes to new depths of prayer. They showed us how prayer can be like a 'hot line' to God. When one of them prayed in tongues, the other would interpret, they seemed to hear directly from God. Jennie told us how she had been determined to hear God's voice, so she sat every day for a week. At first she heard the bird's singing, and the noise of the cars and the people going past, but she persisted and eventually after nearly a week, she heard God speak to her.

Since that special time when I heard God speak to me 'be still and know that I am God', I have not heard such an audible voice, however God has put thoughts and words into my head and spoken through Scripture, pictures and words of knowledge in incredible ways. I have learned that God has different ways to get people's attention, and not everyone will have the same experience. However, if you are prepared to spend time alone with Him, and seek Him with all of your heart, He will draw near to you, and you will have a walking, talking relationship that only comes from time spent with Him.

Bill and Jennie lived by faith, which meant that they relied on gifts of money and for God to supply all of their needs. They told us wonderful stories of how God answered their prayers. One of these was when they were in Papua New Guinea, their young son was desperate to learn to play the piano but they could not afford to buy one. They decided to clear a space in the room and then prayed God would fill the space with a piano! A few days later, there was a knock at the door. An American missionary couple who were returning to the USA told them that they could not take their piano with them, and wondered if Bill and Jennie would like it!

On another occasion their daughter wanted some 'white' roller boots for her birthday. So, as they could not afford to buy any, they prayed about it. Sure enough, within a few days someone came to the door and offered them some roller boots but said that the only problem was they were white! Isn't God good? It made me realise that we need to be specific in our prayers.

Sometimes we forget God knows what we desire, and He longs for us to ask Him. However, He may not always give us what we want, or when we want it! I am reminded of a time when we had been invited to America to stay with the family of Janet (our Minister's wife). We jumped at the chance but gradually the thought crossed our minds that we had not really asked God whether we should go. It would cost a lot of money and should we spend so much on a holiday?

We decided to lay a fleece, and ask God to give us a sign. You may remember when Gideon in the Bible wanted God to give him an answer, he placed a wool fleece on the ground and asked God to ensure that overnight the dew would fall only on the fleece and not on the ground. In the morning he squeezed enough water out of the fleece to fill a bowl, but the ground was dry. Still feeling uncertain, the next night he asked God to do the opposite and sure enough the next day the fleece was dry and the ground was wet. So, we decided to ask God to give us a sign within a week to know whether or not we should go on this holiday. As the week progressed we prayed and read our Bible but did not feel we had an answer. On the Saturday, Janet's parents, who were on holiday in England, came to tea with us. They gave the children a dollar each and said, "you can spend that when you go to America". We told them about our 'fleece' and our desire to know God's leading over this issue. The next day was Sunday, and the week was up that day. We read our Bible before we went to Church and the daily notes referred to Romans 8:32 -

'He who did not spare His own Son but gave Him up for us all – how will He not also, along with Him, graciously give us all things?'

Excitedly, Martyn said, "That's it - that is our answer. He wants to give us all things, including our holiday!" I felt perhaps we should seek further confirmation, and we received this later that morning during the sermon. Bill was preaching on Genesis chapter 22 about Abraham being tested when God asked him to take his son Isaac up the mountain and prepare an altar ready for the sacrifice. The whole sermon was about - 'God will provide' and Bill finished by referring to the same verse we had read earlier in the morning from Romans chapter 8. Now we knew we had our answer, and we were so excited!

That day, some people came to lunch and they just happened to know a Christian Travel Agent, who they said might be able to get us cheaper flight tickets! God really does take care of every detail! It seemed as though, when we were prepared to give up our hearts' desire for God, He did not want us to give it up, only to see whether we were prepared to do so!

We had a wonderful holiday. Janet's parents lent us their car and we drove the 1700 miles round trip to see the Grand Canyon! We could not believe that we were actually standing looking at what man has named as one of the Seven Natural Wonders of the World. We experienced an overwhelming feeling of awe and praise to God, when we watched the sun set and sun rise over the Canyon. As the sun rose in the sky against the backdrop of the black cliffs it bathed the entire Canyon in a blood-red glow. Then its vast walls of rock were transformed into a plethora of spectacular colours. The sun seemed to act like a spotlight picking out the main players on a stage. There was a plaque at one end of the Canyon giving all praise and glory to God for His wonderful creation. Seven year old Paul said, "What a great big hole, whoever could have dug it?" In light of such natural wonders it made me think, how can some people believe that there is no Creator or Master Designer of this world?

Janet's father was part of a team that worked on Apollo 9, 10 and 11, the latter being the spacecraft which landed on the moon in 1969, when astronauts Neil Armstrong and Edwin E. Aldrin Jr. actually walked on the moon. He had such interesting stories to tell, and even had a piece of moon rock in his possession. In recent years there have been television programmes trying to disclaim that men ever walked on the moon. We know from the people we have met it did really happen.

It reminds me of when people say Jesus never came alive again after the crucifixion. The Bible tells us over five hundred people saw Jesus alive, there was no doubt He rose from the dead because they saw him! Maybe in many years to come, when we are dead and gone, people will continue to come up with all sorts of reasons why man could not have walked on the moon, just like they try to come up with reasons why Jesus could not have come alive again. However, if you have any trouble believing either of these events, I do assure you they both happened, and that there are testimonies to prove it. I find it amazing that in school we are all taught about the existence of Julius Caesar, however there is very little evidence about his life and actions in comparison to the amount of historical evidence there is for the life, works, death and resurrection of Jesus Christ. Sadly, most people do not question the existence of Julius Caesar, yet they query the facts about Jesus!

Chapter 8 – Extra-ordinary Prayer Meetings

During the 1980's it was a very exciting time for our Church. The numbers were growing and there was an awareness that God was on the move. We spent a number of holidays together, and enjoyed many family picnics, cricket and football matches. The leadership decided to carry out a survey of the local area, and some of the Church family went from house to house asking various questions, such as: 'Do you read the Bible?', 'Do you go to Church?', and 'Who do you think Jesus was?' The answers were interesting, such as, somebody thought Jesus was an astronaut, and someone else said that they always used the Bible when they had a religious question in the crossword!! There was a tremendous sense of unity within the Church, and I will always remember the excitement when the person arrived back with the 1000th completed questionnaire!

We took part in a number of large outreach events. One of these involved taking over Luton Town Football Ground, for what became an annual event at Christmas time called Carol Aid. Some of us trained up as Counsellors for when Billy Graham came to speak at Wembley Football Stadium. I remember, we were there on a wet, cold evening and I wondered whether anyone would respond to the appeal (Oh ye of little faith!) Once again the Holy Spirit moved amongst the people and thousands went forward to accept Jesus as their Saviour – praise God!

Our Church hired the local sports centre for sports days and Carol Services, which were great opportunities to invite friends, neighbours and dignitaries from the Town Council. One particular event, held at Stopsley Sports Centre, which was of interest to many people, was when the visiting guest just happened to be Cliff Richard! Martyn and I were stewards that evening and Cliff sang and talked about his faith. Just an interesting note here, my brother-in-law John told us that when he was a teenager he attended his local branch of Crusaders each Sunday, and one of the young men who came along to the weekly Bible Studies just happened to be Cliff Richard!

As the Church grew we moved into the local High School for Sunday services. The worship band went from two guitars and three singers to many different musicians, and our weekly worship practices became very special times. We did not just practise new songs we also practised how to worship. We felt we couldn't lead the congregation if we were not worshippers ourselves, which meant not just when we were singing or playing but all the time in our daily lives.

The children's work also grew and I was involved in helping set up a junior music group and drama group, and eventually led some of the monthly family services. I started a Mothers and Toddlers group which became extremely popular and we were able to invite many of these ladies to our family services and outreach functions. God was definitely doing something very special and it was great to be a part of it.

I'll never forget one prayer meeting I was unable to attend! I stayed at home to look after the children, whilst Martyn went to the prayer meeting. I knew that they were praying about whether they should build a new Church and I opened my Bible at Haggai 2:6-9 -

'This is what the Lord Almighty says; 'in a little while I will once more shake the heavens and the earth, the sea and the dry land. I will shake all nations and the desired of all nations will come, and I will fill this house with glory', says the Lord Almighty. 'The silver is mine and the gold is mine', declares the Lord Almighty. 'The glory of this present house will be greater than the glory of the former house', says the Lord Almighty. 'And in this place I will grant peace', declares the Lord Almighty.'

I felt the Lord wanted to speak to the Church, using these verses regarding building a new Church. A few days later, I gave these verses to our Minister and he told me that he had already shared them with the Diaconate and felt this was confirmation. I was so encouraged to think that the Lord had spoken to me through His Word. For those people who say the Bible is just an old-fashioned history book that is not relevant for today - perhaps this will encourage you to realise it is an active, living Word and God still speaks to us through it.

Some land became available next to the High School but it seemed impossible that the Church would be able to have enough money to buy it, let alone put a building on it! As a Church family we had many prayer meetings where God spoke to us through various verses from the Bible. One such passage was felt to be directly from God, in 2 Chronicles chapter 20 where Jehoshaphat was facing the greatest crisis in his life and he began to seek help from the Lord. He said, *"We do not know what to do, but our eyes are upon You"*. (verse 12) The Lord replied, *"Do not be afraid or discouraged because of this vast army. For the battle is not yours, but God's."* (verse 15) Over the months and years that followed, the Church was able to buy the land and also build the beautiful building that stands there today, which has room for many hundreds of people to worship the Lord. Thank you Lord.

Another unforgettable prayer meeting was held at our house the night before Whit Sunday. We had asked permission from our Minister to hold a special prayer meeting, in view of the fact that it was Pentecost – the time we remember when the Holy Spirit came upon the Disciples whilst they were in the upper room in Jerusalem - Acts chapter 2. About fourteen people turned up and after a time of praise, one of the young men told us that he had become a Christian but did not feel any different. He wanted to experience the joy of the Lord, and be filled with the Holy Spirit. Being rather naive, I just laid my hands on his head, and started to pray that the Holy Spirit would come and fill him. I can see him now, sitting in one of our armchairs; the more I prayed "Come Lord Jesus, come and fill him", the more he started gurgling from deep down in his throat. This went on for some time! As I continued to ask Jesus to fill him, the noises grew louder and he threw himself about as though he was having a fit. I had no idea what was happening.

Eventually, after what seemed like ages, a friend of ours, who was a Doctor and a Deacon of the Church, came to my rescue, and sat on the young man! He prayed for peace and everything seemed to calm down. Apart from the fact that a number of the group were terrified and had hidden in the kitchen, and the young man had a very sore throat - the rest of the evening proceeded without further incident!

We found out later that, before he became a Christian, he had been playing with the Ouija board, which is used for obtaining messages in spiritualist séances, and through this he had opened himself up to spirits and demons which were of the Devil. Our Deacon friend told us that because I did not pray for the evil spirit to come out, before asking for the Holy Spirit to fill him, this would explain the terrible noises and battle that went on within him. He also told us that we were fortunate because he had seen some horrible things happen, such as fish and snakes coming out people's mouths and splattering themselves on the wall, or people being very sick, or violent. This was an area we had never been involved in before, and it made us realise that, just as we serve a very real and powerful God, we are in a spiritual battle where the Devil, and the demons and spirits are very much part of this fight.

The following day was Sunday, and by the time we arrived at Church, the news had spread and everyone wanted to know what had happened at the 'Wheeler's' prayer meeting! It occurred to me, that we all go to prayer meetings expecting and wanting God to do something miraculous, and when something happens we seem to be so surprised! The incredible thing was, the young man was transformed and his life was completely changed. He did not have any recollection of what happened, except he felt a great peace, joy and happiness, which he knew could only have come from being filled with the Holy Spirit.

Soon after this event, I read a book called *From Witchcraft to Christ*, by Doreen Irvine, where she tells how she had been involved in drugs and prostitution. She became entangled in the occult, worshipped the Devil and was made a queen of witches. Eventually, Jesus broke through into her life and completely set her free. It is a wonderful testimony showing how God's forgiveness can reach everyone, whatever they may have done, and also a stark reminder of the dangers of dabbling in the occult. I know the story is true because I have a very dear friend who actually knew Doreen personally, and can verify every word. I do not think the average person, let alone Christian, understands the effect of what the occult or spiritual world can have upon us if we start getting involved.

One of the men in our Church worked in a Children's Home and he told us that one day the children had been playing with the Ouija board. When it came to bed time, they rushed up to him and asked if he had a Bible because they were all so frightened they could not sleep. As young as they were, they seemed to think that somehow the Bible would protect them. He found a Bible and spent some time talking to them. After he managed to settle them, he was on his way back downstairs, when he told us that he felt an evil presence pass him. He said, "In the name of Jesus Christ be gone" and at that point, whatever it was, left and the children had a peaceful night.

A friend of mine, whom I met whilst waiting for our children outside the school gates, became very interested in checking out 'spiritual options'. She spent many hours talking to me about Christianity but also went to the local spiritualist Church. One day, the medium said that somebody's dead grandmother wanted to make contact, and pointed to my friend. She told her to go home and sit at her dining room table and her grandmother would be in contact. My friend was terrified, so much so she could not sit at her dining table anymore. She rang me up and asked what should she do? As I had no knowledge of how to help her, I rang our Minister. He informed me that dealings with spiritualism do not bring lasting happiness and often cause fear and depression, and that healings are usually temporary. Also, any voices that appear to be our loved ones are in fact the Devil who can mimic the dead people's voices. Having told my friend this, we prayed together, and she was able to sit at her dining room table without fear.

In the following weeks, she and her husband started coming to our housegroup, but sadly, to our knowledge, they did not make a commitment to follow Jesus. I say 'to our knowledge' because we never know what seeds we have sown in people's lives. Over the years, we have spent many hours talking about the Bible, and Jesus, to different groups of people, and in most cases we do not know what happened to them; but one day we trust we will see them again in Heaven. One man, I recall, was particularly difficult, in that he wanted to disrupt every meeting by asking questions, not necessarily because he wanted answers but just to trip us up. Many years later, we received a letter from him, apologising for being so difficult, and informing us that he had become a Christian, and was now a Deacon in his Church. Isn't God good?

Chapter 9 – Spring Harvest

It was not only an exciting time for the Church, but also for us as a family. We had the privilege of enjoying the ministry of an excellent Minister - and Steve and Janet also became good friends of ours. Steve liked to play snooker and table tennis with our son Paul. In the latter, he often allowed him to reach twenty points to nil - then just as Paul was celebrating his victory, Steve spent the next few minutes claiming the points to eventually win the game! He taught Paul the Latin verb, 'amo' - 'to love'. Someone asked him, "So what does that mean?" and Paul took great delight in saying "It means to mow the grass!" Obviously, Steve had a huge influence on young Paul's life. At five years old he knew exactly what he wanted to be when he grew up - either a Baptist Minister or a snooker player! Thirty years later (with a lot of water having gone under the bridge) Paul is brilliant at pool and snooker and training to be a Baptist Minister!

Steve became involved in the leadership of Spring Harvest and, as a Church, we were encouraged to attend each year. Spring Harvest is an interdenominational event, held at Easter time, at various Holiday Camps throughout the UK. In those days, people would go for a week to enjoy teaching, worship and to use all the facilities of the Holiday Camp. Our first week at Spring Harvest in 1983 was a mixture of shock and pleasure! We were in the older, smaller site at Pontins, Prestatyn, which rather resembled the camp at Colditz! The chalets were basic, cold and draughty. We went to bed wearing extra layers of clothes, and during the day we walked around with so many jumpers, leg warmers and body warmers that we looked like Teletubbies in wellington boots (the latter because of the mud!) However, despite all the cold, and the basic amenities, we loved our times at Spring Harvest.

Those early days were like a taste of Heaven here on earth. Everywhere we went on site there were Christians and it felt so safe, and the children were able to play outside without fear. We were able to spend time with many of our Church fellowship having picnics and fun together. There was no TV except the Christian broadcast which was set up and relayed into the chalets from reception. The worship was led by Graham Kendrick and Dave Pope, and it was our first experience of singing in a Big Top, with hundreds of people all from different denominations. It was an entirely new experience but one which we would repeat many times in the years to come.

Claire and Paul enjoyed their groups and saw many miracles happen amongst the children. It was at Spring Harvest, when Paul was eight years old, that he gave his life to Jesus. He was in a group called the Glorie Company with 1000 children aged 8-11, led by Ishmael (Rev. Ian Smale) and Timmy (now known as Tim Jupp from the well-known Christian band - Delirious!) Paul had been experiencing tooth-ache, and the leaders were praying for children to be healed. He asked someone to pray for his toothache and they said, "Are you a Christian?" to which he replied, "No, but I'd like to be". (He had always said he would not become a Christian just because his Mum and Dad were!) When we collected him after the meeting, he excitedly told us that he had become a Christian and received healing from his toothache. Thank you Lord.

Some years later, when Paul was thirteen and at Spring Harvest Minehead, he was allowed to be a 'helper' in the Glorie Company. Each evening, the leaders covered a different subject, and this particular evening was about the Holy Spirit. An eight year old little girl asked Paul to pray with her to receive the Holy Spirit. This he did, and to his amazement she fell down on the floor under the power of the Holy Spirit.

The next night, the evening was about healing, and she asked him again to pray for her. This time he called a leader to help - you see this little girl had one leg which was one and a half inches shorter than the other and she wore a special boot to compensate. He felt her request was too big for him to take on alone. The leader took off the boot and prayed, and when they opened their eyes the leg had grown to almost the length of the other one! She said, "Come on let's pray some more" and the leg grew to exactly the same length. Later, I asked Paul if he had seen it grow but he said he'd closed his eyes! Perhaps we should all learn to pray with our eyes open to see God in action! At the end of the meeting, the little girl's father came to pick her up, and she rushed to show him what God had done and they danced around the room together rejoicing. The great thing was that Martyn, who was working in the Administration Office, had been sent to deliver a message just as all this was happening, so he had the privilege of witnessing their excitement. The next day the parents took their daughter into Minehead to buy her first 'proper' pair of shoes. God is so good.

The year we went to Spring Harvest at Pwllheli was particularly memorable for me. Four weeks prior to going I fell and broke my wrist. The hospital put a plaster on but gave me an appointment to return in three weeks, instead of the usual six. When the plaster was removed they found that my wrist was still swollen, and painful. The Doctor said it would need another plaster. I was keen to go swimming at Spring Harvest, so I asked if he could just bandage it, and maybe re-plaster it after the holiday! Reluctantly he agreed, giving me all sorts of reasons why it was not a good idea, and so I arrived at Pwllheli with a very painful wrist.

We decided to attend the seminars led by Gerald Coates on Signs and Wonders. A gentleman came to sit next to me, and unfortunately he was a very 'loud' person! When Gerald Coates came onto the stage and said "Good morning everybody", this man next to me shouted "Good morning Gerald". Do you ever get those 'uncomfortable' feelings about people? I'm afraid I felt that way towards him! Especially so, when at the end of the meeting Gerald asked people to stand who wanted to receive the gift of healing. You guessed it - my 'friend' beside me was first up! Those who remained seated were asked to join hands and pray. His wife reached out to take my hand and I said, "Please be careful as I have a broken wrist". I laid my hand on hers and as we prayed I was aware of heat radiating between our palms. I can only describe it as when a hover mower glides over the grass and doesn't appear to touch it. In the same way, our hands were separated by what seemed to be a layer of heat. I kept thinking, something is going on!

When Gerald had finished praying for the people standing, I withdrew my hand and realised that I had full movement and could move it without pain. It was healed. I showed Martyn and then told the lady. She said that she had been praying God would heal me. Her husband said to her, "Perhaps you should have stood up, instead of me" and then laughed saying, "Still God has obviously given you the gift of healing anyway". He did not annoy me this time, as I was too overwhelmed with praise and thanks to God.

We attended Spring Harvest for nine years altogether; we felt the annual spiritual input for our children was so important. Martyn and I voluntarily worked for five years over the different sites, mainly at Butlins, Minehead, although we did go to Skegness one year. By this time many of the chalets had been modernised and as Martyn worked in the Administration Office he usually was privileged to be given one of the better chalets. Unfortunately, there was a mix up in the accommodation at Skegness and, as I was working with the children, I did not qualify for such luxury, so we were given a rather old, cold and damp chalet. It faced towards the North Sea and the cold March wind blew directly through the two inch hole under the front door! We managed to stuff it up with pillows, but it certainly was a test of endurance! One day Chris Bowater, the worship leader, came for lunch with us; however, the next day he was ill with an ear infection. We always wondered if sitting in our draughty chalet had been the cause!

It was so good to have the opportunity to pray with people and help them. One year, Paul took a friend with him who forgot to take his asthma medication. He had a severe asthma attack and we were able to pray with him. He recovered and never had another attack again! Praise the Lord. One evening, following the meeting in the Big Top, there were not enough counsellors to pray with people, so Martyn was asked to go and help. He sat down to pray with a man and his first words were, "So, tell me about the problem you have with your business". The man looked astonished and asked "How did you know I have problems with my business?" Obviously, Martyn had no idea but God did, and they were able to pray together, and the man was amazed and comforted to know God cared for him and his business troubles (and Martyn was thrilled to think God had used him and spoken into the situation).

Our Minister, Steve was on the Executive Committee of Spring Harvest and led many of the main Bible Teachings in the Big Top. I remember one year, our group from Luton all cheered when he came onto the stage, and one lady asked if he was our Minister. When I confirmed that he was, she said, "You are so blessed to have him, he really brings the Bible alive". Due to his connections, we were privileged to have many excellent well-known speakers come to our Church to preach, such as Clive Calver, Steve Chalke, Rob White and Graham Kendrick, to name but a few. At Spring Harvest we would hear such preachers as R. T. Kendall, John Wimber, Roger Forster, Winkie Pratney, Tony Campolo. The list is endless. There were so many gifted young ministers back in the 1980's and 90's it was exciting to think that we were part of their journey, as well as them being a part of ours.

One year we went to the seminars for those in leadership, led by Jim Graham. How we loved listening to his soft Scottish voice, and hearing great wisdom and truths being taught by him. Particularly, I remember he told us that he had been a Minister in a Church for twenty years before being baptised in the Holy Spirit, and indeed it was two years after that when he found himself (to quote) 'pouring out his soul in a language that he had never learned'.

It seems to me that Christians, and even Ministers, can function without this baptism or infilling, anointing, second blessing of the Holy Spirit (whatever you wish to call it). However, everyone who does receive the Holy Spirit in this way, talks about a release of love, joy, peace and power in their lives that was not there before.

I don't know why some people do or do not speak in tongues, or indeed why some are healed and some are not. I think we have to acknowledge God is Sovereign and ask for His will to be done. What we are asked to do is seek to have a closer relationship with the Lord and allow Him, by His Holy Spirit, to make us more like Jesus every day. Our Pentecostal friends say that speaking in tongues is 'the' sign that you have been filled with the Holy Spirit and it is for everyone. We have Christian friends of all denominations who have never spoken in tongues, yet are definitely filled with the Holy Spirit. All I know is, I used to feel a second-class Christian but when I was baptised or filled with the Holy Spirit, my life was completely changed, and I had a passion and a longing for God I did not seem to have before. I was no better than anyone else because of the experience, but I'm so glad God allowed me to see that there was much more that He wanted to give me.

From my own experience, I can only encourage all who read this book to seek God for all that He longs to give you.

Chapter 10 – God's Protection

Looking back over the years, I now realise that God was protecting me long before I was aware of it. My mother loved to tell the story of how, when I was about three years old, I decided to climb out of the first floor bedroom window. I have a vague recollection of climbing along the window sill, holding onto the fanlight window and back into the bedroom through the open window. I was blissfully unaware that below was only a glass conservatory roof to catch me!

On another occasion, when I was about five, I was walking behind my oldest sister, Valerie, in the golf links near our house in Harrow. (Northwick Park Hospital is now where the golf-links used to be!) She was pushing our cousin in the pushchair, and I was wandering along behind, when a man appeared from the other side of a small stream. He asked me if I would like some sweets. I was just about to go towards him when Valerie turned and screamed at me to come back and she marched me off home. My father drilled it into us never to talk to strangers; however, typically I had not heeded his warnings! Why did Valerie turn just at that moment? Some might say it was coincidence. Personally I don't believe in coincidences, only 'God incidents!'

In later years, there were a number of occasions that stand out in my mind, which showed God's supernatural protection. Our Assistant Minister, Bill eventually went to work for a Christian book company in Winchester, before moving to Yorkshire to be Pastor of a Church there. Three times we went to visit them, and on each occasion something happened! We always prayed for God's protection before we set off on a journey and this day was no exception. We were travelling in the middle lane of the motorway, passing a large articulated McDonalds' lorry. As we drew level with it, a piece of metal, approximately two foot six inches square, fell off. Instead of falling on the car, it dropped to the ground, and bounced around the car, eventually coming to rest in the middle of the fast lane of the motorway.

We can only believe that an angel had something to do with it, as in natural terms it was impossible for this piece of metal not to have landed on us. I had never thought much about angels looking after us. I believed God sent angels many times in the Bible to minister help and deliver messages, but what about today?

Hebrews 1:14 says *'Are not all angels ministering spirits sent to serve those who will inherit salvation?'*

On our second trip to Winchester, we were again driving in the middle lane of the motorway when suddenly we saw a wheel bouncing towards us! It must have come from a lorry on the opposite side of the road, but as it bounced over the central reservation barrier it seemed to be gaining speed, and was coming straight towards our car. Again, there had to be some sort of Heavenly intervention, as the wheel suddenly took a completely different course and came to rest at the side of the road.

When we visited Bill and Jennie in Yorkshire, we knew God protected us once more. On the journey there, we were in the fast lane of the M1 behind a number of cars all travelling at about 70 m.p.h., when suddenly the cars ahead braked and the car directly in front of us hit the car ahead and went over on two wheels. It looked as though it was going to turn over but bounced back on to four wheels again. There just happened to be enough space in the middle lane for us to pull over to avoid having a crash!

On the way home, we were travelling along the motorway in the middle lane in the dark! There was little traffic about, and we were aware that a car passed us which had two children's bikes strapped to the back of the boot. Not long afterwards, a car travelling extremely fast flew past and suddenly we saw it spin round and hit the barrier. At the same time, we saw one of the bikes was lying in the middle lane, right in front of us, and to our left on the inside lane was an articulated lorry. We were doing 70 m.p.h. and had nowhere to escape. Thankfully, the driver saw the problem and moved over to the hard shoulder, allowing us to move into his lane and safely bypass the bike. We really were so grateful to God for his protection, but needless to say, we have not visited Bill and Jennie since!

I am reminded of a time when we were very aware of God's protection, but this time we were not travelling. The Church had appointed a young youth leader, from London Bible College. Martyn and I, together with our children, accompanied him, plus four other leaders and about nine young people from the Youth Group to go on a Beach Mission to Torquay, Devon. Our base was at Upton Vale Baptist Church, where we slept on the floor and each day we went to the seafront giving out leaflets and sharing our faith. We invited people back to the Church cafe in the evenings, so the young people, who were aged fourteen to sixteen, could talk to them about Jesus. However, a group of drug addicts and alcoholics came into the cafe, and unfortunately the young people were out of their depth, and very frightened.

We felt we were in a spiritual battle. Martyn and I only stayed for three nights, but we were able to get alongside these men. One man said to Martyn, "If the first thing you tell me is that Jesus loves me, I'll hit you". He replied, "It would not be the first thing I tell you, but He does!" Needless to say, the man did not hit him!

We were moving on for a week's holiday somewhere else, and the group was staying an extra day, but before we left, we were aware that there were relational problems amongst the leaders and also the young people. God gave Martyn a picture of a train track and the train had been diverted into a siding. He shared, with both groups separately, that he felt they had gone to Torquay to do something for God, yet because of relationship problems amongst the group, and the fact that the addicts came in each evening, they had been side-tracked from their original purpose. Both groups put right their differences and God did something very special in each of their lives. That night, as the men were leaving the cafe, they said to Martyn, "See you tomorrow" but Martyn was able to say that we were leaving the next day. He was surprised when the roughest looking man of the group turned to shake his hand and said that he had enjoyed talking to him.

We shall never know what seeds were sown, but we certainly felt God was protecting us throughout that week, both spiritually and physically. The great news was, as we left on that final night, the men did not come back, and two people who came into the cafe gave their lives to Jesus.

Chapter 11 – Friends for a Season

When Paul was about fourteen, he decided to go to a different Church in Luton. He had some friends there, and was friendly with the Pastor's sons. We felt that it would be wrong to prevent him, and on occasions we went with him. The Church had a fantastic worship band and on Sunday nights many young people attended the services. We realised that many people were becoming Christians and being baptised but we felt that there was a need for these people to join Discipleship Courses and to learn more about the Christian faith.

Over a period of nearly two years we felt God was telling us to leave Stopsley Baptist Church and go to Luton Christian Fellowship (LCF). This was an Elim (Pentecostal) Church that believed in much the same doctrine as the Baptists but put more emphasis on using the spiritual gifts (particularly speaking in tongues) described in 1 Corinthians Chapter 14. We had received such good teaching and training we felt that we wanted to help another fellowship. This really was an extremely hard decision to make. It meant leaving a Church family we had known and loved for fifteen years. We were housegroup leaders, led Bible Studies and Discipleship Courses, and new people's groups - at one time nearly every new person who came into the Church came through our group. I was in the worship band and headed up 'the Light Factory' which was a modern way of doing Sunday School for about ninety, five to eleven year olds. You can maybe understand why it took us two years to go, but we felt sure that God was guiding us in this move.

The Pastor at Luton Christian Fellowship was Alan West. He used to play football for Luton Town and England and he would say that he had lived a typical footballer's life! He tells a fantastic story of how he and his wife Cathy were not interested in God but they went on holiday to New Zealand to visit Cathy's parents. Apparently, prior to their holiday, her parents' Church was praying for them to become Christians. The night before they were due to come back to England they became Christians, were baptised and filled with the Holy Spirit. On returning home, they started attending Church and after a number of years Alan became the Pastor. What a wonderful testimony of how God can transform people's lives!

We were at LCF over ten years and God used us in leadership in similar ways as He had done at Stopsley. Martyn became a Deacon and was in charge of the welcome team. He also started a group where men could be accountable to each other, sharing together on a regular basis. I led a weekly Bible Study for ladies, which was a very precious time, where ladies were able to openly learn, share, laugh and cry together.

Over the years, we look back at the special relationships we had within the various groups and realise that, just as we go through seasons in our lives, God also gives us friends for a season, and one day we are looking forward to meeting up with them all again.

I recall one such couple who were in our housegroup. They had four children (three of whom were teenagers) and a young granddaughter, who was the result of their oldest daughter becoming pregnant. Eighteen months later, this same daughter was raped and one evening we received a phone-call from her parents to say that she had taken an overdose. They were not sure whether she would live, and she was rushed to intensive care. Martyn went straight to the hospital to be with them, and I phoned a few people to ask them to pray. By the next day, she had recovered but, because she couldn't give any guarantees that she would not try to take her life again, the hospital transferred her to a secure wing of the hospital.

The next evening, we were due to attend the first of a ten-week course run by the evangelist J. John, called 'Just Ten'. It was held in a refurbished cinema, which had been taken over by a Church, and was situated in the middle of a large Muslim-populated area in Luton. 'Just Ten' is an up-to-date way of looking at the Ten Commandments and applying them to our lives today. As we were leaving home, we received a phone-call to say that our friend's daughter was discharging herself and would her parents go and collect her. They agreed, on the condition that she attended the evening. She arrived and sat beside me. At the end of the meeting, when J. John asked if anyone would like to give their life to the Lord, she went forward for prayer and became a Christian.

Unfortunately, she had not received any counselling following the rape, and whenever she went into the Arndale Shopping Centre in Luton, particular groups of young men threatened and bullied her. She was a very good-looking girl, and she was terrified she would be raped again. Her mother felt that she needed to get away for a few months and go to stay with her grandmother in Honduras, where she would be amongst Christians. To cut a long story short, along with another couple, we helped to buy the air tickets so that she could go as soon as possible, and within days, she and her little daughter were on their way. We felt God used us to help that family in their time of need.

It was not all plain sailing for them after that. The couple had marriage difficulties, problems with their other teenage children, and at one time they sold up everything and went to live in Honduras, in South America, only to come back within six months with no money and nowhere to live! Years later, we were invited to a Church service where they renewed their marriage vows, they were leaders in the Church, their oldest daughter was working with the young people and all their children were walking with God. How blessed we were to be involved in their lives.

It may seem that I have only re-counted the success stories; however we were involved with some very sad events in people's lives. Particularly, I remember Annie, who was only twenty-one years old. She was a student and lived in Luton, and was a member of our housegroup. She had been complaining of pain in her back for a few weeks, and one day felt so sick she took herself to A and E at Luton and Dunstable Hospital. She was admitted for tests and told that she had terminal cancer. The Church started praying and her side ward at the hospital was a mass of flowers and cards. We ensured she had lots of visitors, but in the end she went home to be with her parents, where she died within three weeks. We will never know why such a young, lovely girl was not healed, but she was an inspiration to us all. She knew that she was going to be with Jesus and was looking forward to seeing Him. Sometimes, I think we get so pre-occupied with this life, we forget to get excited about where we're going. We are here on this earth for such a short time in comparison to eternal life. This is just a training ground for what is to come!

At one stage, our housegroup included a number of families who had immense needs. (I have changed their names to protect their identity.) It was a few days before Christmas and we met at Peter and Jane's house. I went into the kitchen to help make the coffee and when Jane opened her kitchen cupboard, I saw it was almost empty. At that point, she broke down in tears and told me that her husband gambled and drank, and often she did not have enough money to feed herself and her two boys.

The next day I spoke to our Minister and explained the situation. He told me to go shopping on behalf of the Church and buy food for the family. This I did and was also able to buy some small Christmas presents for the boys. That night Martyn and I took the food parcel to the house, along with our old small snooker table. Jane burst into tears of joy. However, her husband was angry and at first refused to accept the gifts. He was very proud and said he did not want our charity. Eventually, when he realised that his children would have no food or presents for Christmas day he changed his mind. In the weeks that followed, we were able to get alongside Peter and Jane and with God's help we saw some great changes take place in their lives.

Jane introduced me to a friend of hers who lived across the road. She had huge problems, including having a very violent temper which resulted in her strangling her cat. Also Social Services removed her two children from her for a while because she had pushed one of them down the stairs. Occasionally, when she was angry, she would hurl plates across the kitchen at her husband. One day, whilst visiting, I noticed she had no plates left, having smashed them all! We were able to replace them with some free plates we had collected from vouchers from our local garage. (At one time, the garage gave vouchers with petrol, which could be exchanged for plates and we had saved more than enough for an entire dinner service!) However, I gave the plates to her with strict instructions they were not to be thrown across her kitchen!

I started a Discipleship Course with her and she did give her life to Jesus, but because of her lifestyle and debts she did not find life easy. She said that whilst I was with her, she was aware of God's presence and she was able to manage, but as soon as I left, everything went wrong again. One evening Martyn and I called to see her, and the house was very cold. Apparently, her husband had used their last few pounds to go out for a drink, leaving no money to put in the meter for electricity. We were really bothered that the children would wake up next morning to a cold house and no breakfast, so we went home and returned with some money to feed the meter.

One night, she phoned me to say that she was going to take the car and crash into a wall to end her life, if I did not go and see her immediately. I phoned our Doctor friend, who was a Deacon of the Church and he advised me not to go. He said that in his experience, people who talk about suicide rarely do it. I spent a very fretful night, wondering whether I should have gone to see this lady, and 'what if she carried out her threat?' However, next morning when I rang her, she was still there! A few days later however I called to see her, and found no one lived there anymore. They had packed up and gone, leaving no forwarding address.

We never knew what happened to that little family. We can only pray that through our sharing the love of Jesus with them in practical ways, one day they might have a real relationship with Jesus for themselves and their lives will be transformed.

Chapter 12 – Trials

I called this book, *Trials, Signs and Wonders* for a reason. I have shared many of the wonderful things that God has done in our lives, however we have not been exempt from our fair share of trials! There are those people who think that Christians are entitled to be blessed and that they should not suffer. I cannot believe that this is the case. If we look at Paul in the Bible, in the Book of Acts, he suffered more than most – he was imprisoned and beaten many times, stoned and bound in chains, ship-wrecked three times, and these are just some of his sufferings! None of us enjoy trials, but looking back I know God was there with us through the tough times and teaching us along the way.

In the early 1990's Martyn went through a very difficult period with his job as a Building Society Manager. The company decided to get rid of Managers who were over forty, in favour of younger men. There was a great deal of pressure on the staff to 'sell' mortgages, credit cards, endowments and unsecured loans and Martyn did not feel right about doing this. (In later years, we have seen what a mess the Financial Institutions created by following these policies.) He decided to look for another job and became a Financial Advisor. He had only left the Building Society six weeks, when he found out that all Managers who were over forty years old were being offered redundancy packages and because of his long service he would have received over £30,000! Unfortunately, the new job did not live up to its promises - or at any rate the promises the boss had made to him!

Life at work was very hard. Instead of being a Manager in charge of staff who were mainly women, he found himself in an office of young, ambitious men who were cut-throat, and goal-orientated. He worked long hours, over and above normal office hours, and travelled all over the country visiting clients. He did enjoy some parts of the job: attending the Money Show in London, cruising for a few days on the QE2 (all expenses paid), dinners at the Ritz and Grosvenor House Hotels in London, playing in golf competitions, going for a weekend to The Glen Eagles Hotel, in Scotland (again all expenses paid - and this time I was able to accompany him as well!) Unfortunately, the perks did not outweigh the difficulties. The incredible provision of God was that the only year Martyn met his targets, and received a bonus, was the year that Claire was married, and the extra money paid for her wedding. Thank you Lord.

Whilst we were in Jamaica celebrating our 25th wedding anniversary, I shared with Martyn that I felt the Lord wanted him to leave his job and become a childminder. I had been running a successful childminding business for about ten years and, whilst praying about his work situation, the Lord gave me various verses from Isaiah, encouraging him to leave.

Verses such as Isaiah 52:12 - *'You will not leave in haste or go in flight; for the Lord will go before you, the God of Israel will be your rear guard'*, and chapters 44-46 - most of the verses seemed to jump out at me! I know that it is not a good idea to take verses out of context, but through these verses I believed very strongly that God was telling Martyn to leave his job. However, at that time, he would not even contemplate becoming a childminder.

Over the next few months the situation at work became even more difficult, and nine months later Martyn caught a flu-like virus which was the beginning of ME (myalgic encephalomyelitis) or post viral fatigue syndrome, which attacks every muscle in the body. He was tremendously tired, and could hardly walk upstairs, or to the bottom of the garden. He was constantly in a lot of pain, especially in the calves of his legs. He could not concentrate enough to read and just kept flicking through the programmes on the television. Also, large red 'boil-like' spots came out all over his body, which was the start of psoriasis. Martyn prayed that none of the spots would come on his face, and praise the Lord they never did.

He was beginning to feel like Job in the Bible who came out in boils, lost everything, yet still trusted God throughout it all. Martyn did not have any long-term sickness plan in his contract at work, and after six weeks his boss took away his car and stopped paying him. I remember one of the ladies from Church rang me up and said, "How awful it must be for you" and "are you able to cope?" Amazingly, we had great peace and knew God was in control of everything. We completely trusted Him and knew He would provide.

About this time, I was due for my annual inspection from Social Services regarding the childminding business. The lady who visited me was a Christian and each year I looked forward to her coming. When she heard Martyn was off work sick, she told us that because he was in the house whilst the children were there, he must be registered as a childminder. So it happened, just as God had told me! As soon as he became a childminder, the phone never stopped ringing from people wanting to have their children looked after. At first, he could only sit on the settee all day and hold the babies, but at least we were able to take on more children which helped pay the bills.

By Christmas, the psoriasis was so bad that the Doctor decided to send Martyn to a Consultant, who took a biopsy of one of the spots. His boss was being particularly difficult and wrote to our Doctor, asking him when Martyn would return to work. Our Doctor took great delight in charging him fifty pounds to reply, telling him that he had no idea when Martyn would be fit to work again. However, Martyn decided to hand in his notice and at that point the spots disappeared! When he returned for the result of the biopsy, the Consultant was amazed that the spots had completely gone!

Three months later, Martyn was sitting in Church listening to Alan West preaching about the miracles of Jesus. He thought of all the miracles that we had seen in our lives and he said to himself, 'Jesus is still doing miracles today'. At that point, he felt what seemed like a ball of fire go through his body, from his toes to his head and the pain went from his legs. God had completely healed him. No one laid hands on him, in fact at that point no one prayed for him (although he had been prayed for previously). After this, Martyn had many opportunities to tell people about his healing. At first, our Doctor was very sceptical and he gave Martyn a medical note for another month, just in case! When he returned and told the Doctor that he had walked the length of Oxford Street in London, played golf and tennis, and felt fitter than he had done for years, the Doctor had to accept that Martyn had been healed.

When he was in the school playground waiting for some of our childminding children, often mothers would ask which child he was waiting for. This opened up opportunities to talk about how he came to be a childminder and about his healing. One funny reaction came from a lady who said "I know all about healing, we once had a rabbit that was healed!" One of the fathers who often collected his children from school was Lee Dixon, the footballer who played for Arsenal Football Club, and Martyn enjoyed chatting and sharing with him.

We often wondered - if Martyn had given up work when God first spoke, would he have avoided all that pain and illness? God alone knows! Walking with God is a learning process. We have not always found it easy to detect God's leading, and walk in complete faith and obedience, but when we did, the joy and peace that came was incredible. It was hard for Martyn to give up the security of a job and being the provider for the family. However, he would admit now that when he was a childminder, it was the happiest time of his working life and certainly we earned more money working together than he ever earned in the financial world! He often said that being a childminder was rather like being a financial consultant - you did everything for the clients financially and looked after all their needs, but obviously did not change their nappies! We not only enjoyed working together but loved the opportunity to mould and develop the little lives we had in our care. Many of the children were with us from small babies, until they went to High School and indeed we still keep in touch with some of them today (nearly twenty years later!)

One thing I need to say. We all ask "why does God heal one person and not another?" We will not know the answer to that until we get to Heaven! At the same time as Martyn was ill, a very good Christian friend of ours also had ME. She had two young children, a beautiful singing voice, did a lot of work in the Church, and she became so ill she could not even look after her husband, home or children. Many years later, we met her again, and after years of illness she was able to work, but was still not completely healed. Why was Martyn healed and not her? I have come to understand that God is Sovereign and He alone knows why and we can only thank and praise Him for what he did for us.

A very sudden and sad event in our life was when my father died. On Monday September 23rd 1996 he rode his bicycle to collect his prescription and pension, as he had done so many times before. As he set off for home, he sadly did not look and turned straight into the path of an oncoming taxi. The collision was unavoidable and my father was tossed up onto the bonnet of the car and came down on the road, leaving him with two very badly broken legs. An ambulance was called and he was taken to Brighton Hospital. My mother telephoned to tell me what had happened and I offered to go straight away to see him. However, she assured me that there was no need, so I made plans to visit him at the weekend. The next phone call I received from my mother was two days later to say that my father had died of a pulmonary embolism. How I regretted not going straight away. It seemed very hard that I was not able to say goodbye, and this really did bother me for quite a while.

Although my childhood had been tough, I look back and realise that my father had taught me so much and I have many good memories of him. Our children, Claire and Paul also remember the good times they spent with their grandfather. They enjoyed long walks in the woods with him and his dog, and Paul and his grandfather would play snooker together for many hours. At the funeral it was good for all the family to get together - including my middle sister Kitty and her husband and children. (We had been unable to all be together at my parents' house for a long time because my father could not cope with a lot of people being around him.) Indeed, following the funeral we had many happy family reunions. It seemed ironic that, as the oldest member of the family had just passed away, there in our midst was seven week old, Nathan, our first grandchild. I was reminded of the verses in Ecclesiastes where it says:

Ecclesiastes 1:4:- *'One generation goes its way, the next one arrives, but nothing changes – it's business as usual for old planet earth!'* (taken from *The Message* version of the Bible)

Ecclesiastes 3:1-2 – *'There is a time for everything, a time to be born and a time to die.'*

I think funerals tend to make us realise how vulnerable we are and that life as we know it will not go on indefinitely. Perhaps it is the only time some people think about death. We seem to put to the back of our minds that one out of one people will die! It has been said that 'there are only two places where we will spend eternity – Heaven or Hell - which one will we choose?'

Chapter 13 – Strange Happenings

During the 1990's we were exposed to something completely new spiritually. Many people will have heard of the Toronto Blessing which originated from the Toronto Airport Vineyard Church. It was said that God was visiting his Church in a fresh and new way. Actually, we knew nothing of what was happening, but around this time a group from Church decided to attend a two-day worship conference at Holy Trinity Brompton, which is a charismatic evangelical Anglican Church in London. John Wimber was the speaker, and having heard him speak at Spring Harvest, Martyn and I decided to attend.

We were completely unprepared for what we saw and heard that day. Things happened during the worship that shocked us. All we could do was watch what happened to the people around us. The Church building is quite old and has large pillars supporting the roof. One person spent the entire time trying to climb up one of these pillars, a rather large lady rolled from the back of the Church to the front, some cried, some laughed, and one person just ran on the spot! Another person continuously shook her head violently, another roared like a lion, and one man just shook all over throughout the worship.

Indeed, when we went into McDonalds for our lunch, Martyn saw this person in the queue and he whispered to me that he hoped the man did not start shaking whilst drinking his milk shake! We went home, very worried. We had been led to believe that, just like the Holy Spirit wants to do miraculous signs and wonders amongst us, the Devil can also mimic and copy and we need discernment to know whether it is of God or not. That night I prayed God would let us know if any of this was from Him.

At the start of the next day, John Wimber invited people to give their testimonies from the previous day! The lady who had been shaking her head involuntarily, shared that for some time she had been troubled by a neck and shoulder problem and had not been able to move her neck. Following what happened in the worship she was completely healed and now had full movement. Regarding the lady who had been roaring like a lion, John Wimber explained such things were a prophetic symbol of the anger of the Lion of Judah (mentioned in the Bible) roaring over the injustices in the Church and in our world. He certainly did not explain the rolling, or the climbing or the shaking, but he did make us worry when he said "Who are we to query if God wants to do a new thing in our generation?" and "we should not really question it!"

I believe God may want to do a new thing with us, however it always must be in line with His Word, the Bible, and also any 'experience' should make a difference in our lives, so we can point others to Jesus, and be more Christ-like because of it.

We heard John Wimber was speaking at Wembley Conference Centre, so we encouraged Claire and Paul to go with others from our Church. Sadly, the experience was not a good one. They came home amazed at the 'antics' people got up to. People were screaming, laughing, weeping, clucking like hens, mooing like cows and barking like dogs. Our young people were very disillusioned and really it did more harm than good. I understand in later years before he died, John Wimber did disassociate himself with some of what was going on, but I am afraid that even into the 21st Century we have seen peculiar happenings!

More recently, there was the 'Florida Outpouring' which was widely televised on the God Channel. Many people claimed to be healed and had life-changing experiences, but I noted that many of the methods encouraged by the speakers and worship leaders were very strange. We saw people supposedly worshipping God, but looking more like they were doing a tribal warrior dance, often verging on being in a trance. We heard of people coming back to the UK with what was called 'the anointing'; however, a friend of ours went to Florida in desperate need of healing, and we saw her on the television. She was on the stage with others who were being prayed for, yet nothing happened to her.

We went to a Conference where gold and silver were apparently found on the floor and oil dripped from the speaker's hands. Another time, I went to a 'soaking' meeting where we were asked to clear our minds of everything, which seemed more akin to Eastern meditation. In later years we have come across so many different people with their own interpretations of Scripture, and have met people who believe very strange things - many of whom have fallen out with mainstream Church because they believe that they are right and the Church is wrong.

Due to the fact God has done miraculous things in our life, we have tried to remain open to what God wants to do and not prevent Him from working because of our unbelief. However, we have struggled with many of these things that have been happening and are reminded of the words of Jesus in Matthew 24:10-11 when He talks about signs of the end times -

'At that time many will turn away from the faith and will betray and hate each other and many false prophets will appear and deceive many people,'

And Matthew 24:24 - *'For false Christs and false prophets will appear and perform great signs and miracles to deceive even the elect - if that were possible. See, I have told you ahead of time.'*

Chapter 14 – Holidays

For the first few years of our marriage, Martyn and I could not afford a holiday, so we spent most of our summer holidays in Worthing, staying with my parents. However, as the children grew older, I used to work, first as a cleaner and then a childminder, in order to raise enough money for us to go away as a family.

Our first package holiday was two weeks to St. Lucia in the Caribbean. We had a wonderful time and felt very blessed to be there. We met a Christian waiter, who offered to take us to his Church. On the Sunday morning, he picked us up in a mini-bus. He was dressed in his best clothes, long black trousers, with a white shirt with frills, together with a bow tie. It was extremely hot and we felt a little embarrassed that we were only dressed in our shorts and tee shirts! He drove for about half an hour along very narrow dusty bumpy lanes with huge potholes, into the middle of a large banana plantation, where we saw hundreds of trees covered in blue polythene bags that apparently were protecting the green bananas from insects. We were taken to a small building which was overflowing with people who were singing joyfully. On the way, we had passed many people all dressed in their 'Sunday best' walking to Church singing. On one side of the Church sat the English-speaking people and on the other side were those who spoke Patois, the local language. The children met outside for Sunday School in the cow shed!

We read Psalm 121: 1-2 - *'I will look to the hills - where does my help come from? My help comes from the Lord, the Maker of Heaven and earth.'* These words took on a whole new meaning as I looked out of the space where a window should be, at the spectacular view of the green hills and countryside that were wrapped in the radiant light of the hot sunshine, with a canopy overhead of brilliant blue sky. Surely only God - the expert Craftsman - could create such an exquisite masterpiece?

During the service, it was so hot that people in the congregation would slip out at different times during the sermon and put their heads under a cold tap of running water to cool off! It was certainly a very unusual service but the people were very sincere and joyful in their worship. It was wonderful to be so far away from home, yet feel such a part of this little fellowship as we worshipped God together. At the end of the meeting the Minister said "Perhaps our visitors from England would like to say a few words?" Martyn realised that he was looking directly at him, and being the only white man there, knew he had to say something! He brought greetings from our Church fellowship back home, and said that he noticed that there was a sign saying they were raising money to build a new Church and were hoping to reach two hundred and fifty thousand Eastern Caribbean dollars. He then told them that our Church was also raising money for a new Church building but we needed over a million pounds, four times the amount they were aiming for! You can imagine that this little congregation were amazed to hear that it would take so much money to build a Church in England!

On the way back to the hotel, our waiter friend took us to visit his family, who were very poor, but most welcoming. Our son Paul, who was only eleven, had quite a culture shock when he asked to go to the toilet, only to find that it was outside and just a hole in the ground!

Our first holiday away without the family, was when we celebrated our silver wedding anniversary in Jamaica and it seemed strange just being the two of us! We had always enjoyed our family holidays, and even when the children became teenagers it seemed that they still enjoyed holidaying with us! However, there we were on our own, but not for long! We had always prayed for 'Divine appointments' and we soon made friends with a family comprising of Mum, Dad and their two teenage daughters. Apparently, they were having their last holiday together to try to improve their relationships, but it was not working very well! Due to our experiences of the teenage years we were able to share and hopefully help them. We could only pray that on returning home they would continue to want to work at keeping together as a family.

One year, we were on holiday in the Dominican Republic and we met a couple from England, who had just got married and were on their honeymoon (although they had been living together for some time). We spent much of the holiday with them and soon realised that they had relationship problems. Lisa enjoyed reading, and on finishing her book, I offered her one of mine. I had taken a couple of books with me, one of them being *I dared to call Him Father* by Bilquis Sheikh. This tells the story of when Bilquis, an influential Moslem lady, became a Christian and how her family and friends turned against her and the problems that she encountered. I had read the book before, but just felt prompted to take it on holiday with me. Unbeknown to me, Lisa had previously been married to a Moslem man, and after reading the book, she shared with me many of the troubles and difficulties that she had experienced. It helped her to understand, not only about the Moslem faith but also about Christianity. I knew then why I had felt compelled to take that book with me. How I wish I would listen to that still small voice of the Holy Spirit prompting me more often!

Towards the end of the holiday, Kevin and Lisa had a major row, which ended in Kevin telling us that his wife had thrown her wedding ring across the room and told him that the marriage was over. We spent some hours talking to him and encouraged him to go and see Lisa, assuring him we would be praying that they would resolve their differences. He went away, quite sure that our prayers would be a waste of time. Later that evening, we were delighted to see them both walking towards us, hand in hand. God had answered our prayers and we were able to talk to them further about God and the power of prayer.

God has allowed us to enjoy many wonderful holidays, some in Spain, Texas, Florida and the Caribbean, and we have had the privilege of worshipping with God's people in both large and small venues. We joined together with thousands in First Baptist Church Dallas, and hundreds in First Baptist Church Lubbock; both were memorable experiences. We took part in Services on board ship crossing the Atlantic, where on one occasion the sea was so rough we had to remain seated to sing the hymns! A number of times we have enjoyed attending English-speaking Churches in Spain – we found it so encouraging to meet up with God's people from all over the world.

We have great memories of meeting a taxi driver called 'the Godfather!' Whilst cruising in the Caribbean we visited the beautiful island of St. Thomas. The 'Godfather' drove us to a lovely beach called Magens Bay which is on the far side of the island. It is advertised as one of the top ten 'best beaches' in the world and as we travelled along very narrow, steep, bumpy roads we were serenaded on the journey by his Christian music! Martyn got into conversation with him and it transpired that he was a Christian and was very interested in modern English Christian music. He arranged to come back for us in the afternoon saying "When you are ready to leave, just ask a local person for the 'Godfather' – everyone knows me!" Sure enough, this happened and he came back for us and took us to see the most magnificent views of the island, for no extra charge. Ten years later, we returned to St. Thomas and went to the tourist information centre and asked if the 'Godfather' was still around. Imagine our excitement when the lady called him on the phone and we were able to speak to him. Sadly, he was working at a different port but it was wonderful to make contact again. It reminded me that, because of our love of Jesus, one day we will meet up in Heaven with all those Christians whom we have perhaps only met briefly in this world – what a wonderful day that will be!

Our holiday in California particularly stands out in my memory. How we arrived there was a tremendous blessing because, due to a long delay previously with a Virgin flight, we were given enough air miles for a return flight to California! There is no doubt that we would never have been able to go at all, if God had not taken away my fear of flying and dying! I had previously said I would never go to California because of its history of earthquakes! We stayed in Palm Springs and I went horse riding along what appeared to be a dusty, dried up river bed, surrounded each side by rugged mountains. Imagine my surprise when my companion told me not to worry if my horse became rather 'jittery'. He apparently could feel the ground vibrating under his feet constantly with the 'tremors!' We were riding along the San Andreas Fault, which is the 800 mile line where earthquakes are likely to occur at any time! What a good feeling that I knew that my life was in the Lord's hands!

During our stay, we had the free use of a luxury hotel's swimming pool, spa and leisure facilities for a week. It was for adults only, a child-free zone! Although we loved our childminding children dearly, what a restful holiday we had - with not a child in sight!

One day we took a cable car up to the top of a high mountain. We had been warned that the temperature dropped from about 115 degrees to a cool 70 at the top! Of course, that was warm for us English people! The cable car was made of glass and as we ascended, it gave us wonderful panoramic views of the mountains and desert stretching far away into the distance. At the top, we walked through woods full of pine trees and eucalyptus trees with trunks that smelt of vanilla! We sat for ages just drinking in the sights and smells, aware that there was no noise at all - complete silence! It was incredibly peaceful. Suddenly, we heard what can only be described as clapping of hands. We looked around and realised that it was the sound of the wind in the trees, causing the leaves to seem as though they were clapping!

It reminded us of the words in Isaiah 55:12 -

'the trees of the fields will clap their hands;'

It had always seemed such a strange thing to say, until we heard it for ourselves! It just seemed as though even the trees were praising God. We shall never forget that wonderful experience of God's perfect creation.

Chapter 15 – Paul

In the next couple of chapters I shall recall some of the events that were part of Claire and Paul's lives.

The early days at school for Paul were great fun. He loved to make the whole class laugh at him. I remember our very first parents' evening, and his teacher told us that if Paul came into school with 'that twinkle' in his eye, she had lost control of the class for the whole day! At his Junior school, he spent many lunchtimes sitting outside the Headmaster's office for various silly reasons! He was known as 'Pope Paul' for a short period, as in one assembly he contradicted the Headmaster on his Bible knowledge, in front of the whole school! From that time, the Headmaster seemed to be looking for ways to catch him out! My father offered to send Paul to Private School to see if he would settle down and take school more seriously. However, he still tried to be the 'joker' even there, and one of the reports from the Headmaster seemed to sum him up perfectly - 'Never have I met a boy, outwardly so eager to please, yet inwardly determined not to do so!'

At thirteen Paul left the Private School and went to an all boys' State School in St. Albans - and had a very big culture shock. For two years he had been in smaller classes, where the work was almost to GCSE standard. He was astonished to now find himself with much less school-work, and amongst classmates who had a lack of manners and respect, especially for the female teachers. He was a quiet boy who did not swear like the others and, unfortunately, he was bullied by two or three different boys. On one occasion, he arrived at Martyn's office in St. Albans saying that he could not go back to school anymore. Previously, Martyn had noticed bruises on Paul's body but, when questioned, he claimed that he had banged into a filing cabinet. We found out later that he had been deliberately pushed many times. We rang the school and they were fast and efficient in dealing with the situation, threatening the culprits with expulsion if it should happen again.

Paul enjoyed his years in Boys' Brigade, working for his Bronze and Silver Duke of Edinburgh Awards, and playing football for Christians in Sport. However, sadly, he felt that being a Christian at school, and turning the other cheek as it were, had caused him too much pain and trouble. So, when he went to College he mixed with the 'in crowd' and those who were known to be 'the hard lads' and became one of their 'gang'. He didn't have many friends at Church and decided to stop going because in his words, he 'did not want to be hypocritical'. He knew the life that he wanted to lead was against all that he had ever been taught and he didn't want to pretend to be someone he was not! He told our Minister that he was putting God on hold for a while and would perhaps return to Him in later years! The reply came back, "You are a braver man than I am, as there is always that chance you may not have the opportunity to return to God before you die".

Martyn and I prayed regularly with another couple who had a 'wayward' teenager and it really helped to have someone in whom we could confide and share. One day, whilst we were praying together, the lady had a picture of Paul on one of those long extending dog's leads, and God was reeling him in. She felt God was saying that He would allow Paul to go to the end of the dog's lead, before He would draw him back again, and certainly He would never let him go. Also, she said she believed God was saying that one day Paul would be a 'great man of God'.

We hung on to those words through many tough years. Sometimes I had to ask myself, 'did I love him because he did as I wanted him to do - follow my faith, values etc., or did I love him unconditionally, because he was my son?' It was interesting how at that time God brought across our path a number of parents who were struggling with their teenagers and we were able to help them by sharing our experiences. Looking back, it was the most difficult time in our lives but we know God was with us through it all and only now, years later, can we see how God's plans and purposes have been worked out. It is hard for Christian parents to protect their children from the world's ways - the greatest weapon we have is prayer at all times.

Sometimes, I found it very hard to leave it to God - I felt that He needed a helping hand!! There were times when perhaps Paul was meant to be at work and we knew that he was in the pub or the nightclub and we would go out looking for him to bring him home - but it didn't do any of us any good, or make the situation any better. Don't get me wrong, he was never a bad person, no trouble with the police or drugs etc. However, because of our Christian values and principles, the life that he was leading was completely alien to everything we believed in. He loved playing pool and being one of 'the boys' and had a habit of being in the wrong place at the wrong time, and spending money he did not have!

After college, and 'three months' at Luton University, Paul joined a Tennis Academy in St. Albans and qualified with the Lawn Tennis Association as a Tennis Coach. Some months later he went to the John Newcombe Tennis Ranch in Texas, America. He met an American girl and brought her back to England. They stayed with us for four months and then returned to America, where they married and Paul became a Head Tennis Coach in a Country Club in Arkansas. Sadly, the marriage and the job did not last very long! After seventeen months he came home, with no job, and no money. Paul was a bit like the prodigal son - he had to sink to rock bottom in his life before he came to his senses!

A friend from Church asked him if he would go to Spring Harvest at Skegness, with a group of young people. He was far from God at the time but he thought it would be fun to play some football and spend the evenings in the pub! On the final night the leader of the group said to him, "If you will come with me to the evening meeting in the Big Top, I will go to the pub afterwards with you". So, that is what happened. However, Paul did not bargain on God being there! After the meeting, he was sitting thinking about what he had heard and an old man came and tapped him on the shoulder and said "God has told me to tell you that there is a place in Heaven reserved for you". As you can imagine, this made him sit up and think - but not for long!

He managed to get a tennis coaching job in Birmingham, but things did not go too well there - mainly because of his social life! One day whilst out on the tennis court, he tells the story of how he literally heard God say, "I want you to go to Bible College". So, back home to Mum and Dad he came once more - again no job and no money! He shared with us what he felt God had said to him, but as he had not been to Church for years and his lifestyle was far from what it should be, we wondered how this was going to come about. We often said to him that he used God like a magic man. Every time he got into difficulties, he would pray and it was as if that long dog's lead was being pulled in each time to get him out of trouble.

The Head Office of Youth with a Mission (YWAM) is in Harpenden, and they take young people on six months Discipleship Training School (DTS) courses - three months for study and three months practical experience in different parts of the world. Paul thought that this would be a good starting point, but first he had to get a reference from the Pastor of his Church, and second, where was the money coming from? Paul had attended Luton Christian Fellowship for a while, and went to see Alan West. It was a miracle that he gave him a reference and my mother offered to help him financially. Unfortunately, it was not a good idea that he chose a course so close to home. Instead of spending evenings at the base, he continued his social life amongst his friends in Harpenden, and his three months away in Russia did not exactly change his life either! Sadly he must have been one of the few people who failed the course!

However, God did not let go of him. The new Minister of Stopsley Baptist Church, Brian Doyle, took him under his wing, and met with him regularly for a few months. One day Martyn and I met Brian in the Luton Arndale Centre and we thanked him for spending time with Paul. He said that he was glad to do so, as he believed deep down inside Paul was a jewel, and he saw it as his job to bring it out! Brian suggested Paul went on another YWAM DTS course, this time to Cyprus, where he would be teaching. It was whilst in Cyprus that Paul re-dedicated his life to the Lord. Although he had been baptised at sixteen (just before it all kicked off with his 'other' life!) he was baptised again in the Mediterranean Sea - this time as a baptism of repentance. God was beginning to draw in that long dog's lead! After three months 'practical' in Jordan, Paul passed the DTS course, and decided to go for a year to Capernwray International Bible School in Lancashire. Due to his life over the past few years, he had issues to deal with, but God carried on the job of chipping away at that jewel inside him.

Following this, for three years Paul went to Moorlands Bible College in Christchurch, near Bournemouth, and gained a BA Honours in Applied Theology. He then attended Spurgeon's Bible College in London where he gained a Master of Theology in Biblical Studies. All this was only made possible because his grandmother, Nanna Wheatley, was obedient to the Holy Spirit's leading in her life. She has now died of Alzheimer's disease but she used to tell the story of how she was aware God had told her to help Paul through Bible College. She kept saying, "I know what I have to do". God laid this on her heart, and she provided all the finances needed. We thank the Lord for her obedience and generosity which enabled God's purposes and plans for Paul's life to come to fruition.

Just a thought, regarding Alzheimer's disease - this was a time of real trial and sadness for us as a family. To watch our Mum change from being very mentally and physically active, to having the mentality of a baby was extremely hard and painful. My oldest sister Valerie had always lived with my Mum but since they moved to Scotland in 2000, I was only able to visit her every few months. After a while she did not recognise me and indeed only saw my sister as a Carer. Her sweet character continued to the end, and for a long time, even when her mind had gone, she remembered the hymns and nursery rhymes she had sung as a child, and we would sing along together. It is a very cruel disease for the patient, but also for the relatives who can only watch and pray. Three months before our Mum died, Valerie had been concerned about how she was going to cope, as Mum was deteriorating and there were no suitable rooms available in local Care Homes. Around this time, Valerie fell over and injured her shoulder, and was unable to look after Mum at home. Social Services stepped in and found her a temporary room in a local Nursing Home.

We were all praying about the situation and Valerie read John 14:1-3 where Jesus said –

'Do not let your hearts be troubled. Trust in God; trust also in me. In my Father's house are many rooms; if it were not so, I would have told you. I am going there to prepare a place for you, and if I go and prepare a place for you, I will come back and take you to be with me that you may also be where I am.'

It was as if these words jumped out of the page at Valerie. She believed that Jesus was saying to her, "Do not worry - I have prepared a room for Mum". Within a few days, she had been given a permanent room at the Nursing Home, where she stayed until she died three months later. I remember seeing her body lying in the coffin before the funeral, and I knew that she was not there anymore. As Valerie had read, Jesus had promised He would come back to take her to be with Him – she had gone to be with her Jesus.

The Bible says, in Revelation 21:4 - *'He will wipe every tear from their eyes. There will be no more death or mourning or crying or pain, for the old order of things has passed away.'*

We believe our Mum now has a new body, a new mind and a new place to live, and one day we will see her again. Life on this earth was not always happy or easy for Mum, but she knew Jesus was there with her, and trusted Him to the end.

Back to Paul. After gaining his Masters, he was offered an Internship at a large Baptist Church in Texas, America. Unfortunately, due to a problem with a visa when he first went to America some years before, he was prevented from entering the country. The Authorities told him that he would have to return to England on the next available flight, which was not until the following day. Meanwhile, he would have to spend the night in the County Jail (presumably so that he could not escape!) He was handcuffed, dressed in an orange jump-suit and put in jail with a number of very large black guys who were all in for knife and gun crimes. Paul was given a small box containing a toothbrush, toothpaste, soap etc., which (knowing, or hoping, he would not be stopping long) he distributed amongst the inmates. One of them did offer him five dollars to give away his white tee-shirt which he had been allowed to wear under the jump suit, but because the air conditioning was so cold during the night, Paul did not want to part with that! The inmates advised him not to touch the food as it caused 'the runs' - so he neither slept nor ate that night! They acknowledged that they deserved to be in jail because of the crimes they had committed but found it quite comical that he was there for a visa violation!

The next day, the police escorted Paul (still in handcuffs) to the plane, and he was not given his passport back until he reached Heathrow, London. Feeling rather sorry for himself, and certainly very hungry and tired, he prepared himself for the long journey home. Three American guys came and sat by Paul, and started chatting with him. It transpired that they were Ministers on their way to Bangladesh to do some missionary work. After they heard about Paul's adventure, they spent the journey talking about the Bible and theology and the time literally 'flew' by! Paul loves to debate theology, and God provided just the right travelling companions to take the sting out of his 'ordeal'.

Following this 'career' set back, Paul spent some time being unemployed. He had felt so sure God wanted him to go to America to work in a Church there but it now seemed as though that door was very firmly shut. So, where to next, God? An opportunity arose for him to go with a team of people to Nigeria to preach and minister to some Churches there. It was a tremendous experience and he saw God working in supernatural ways in people's lives. When he returned home, an Assemblies of God Church in Brixham, Torbay, gave him a six months internship before Andover Baptist Church gave him a job as their caretaker/cleaner! At the same time, he was given opportunities to preach, lead an Alpha course, teach on an Internship Programme and generally gain the experience he would need to be a Minister himself.

Normally, it takes a couple of years before a Baptist Church will recommend someone to go before a Panel of Ministers to 'test' their 'calling'. However, before a year was over, Paul had gone before the Panel and had been approved to be trained as a Baptist Minister. It was agreed that he attend Regent's Park College, Oxford for two years to go through the Ministers' Accreditation Scheme, which would enable him to become a fully trained Baptist Minister. The problem was, now he needed a Church to sponsor him and take him on as their Minister in Training.

Just before he was due to start at Regent's Park, a small Baptist Church in Whitchurch, Hampshire offered to help support him. God's timing was perfect, as usual! Paul had preached there on several occasions during his time at Andover. This Church dates back to 1652 and has a fantastic history and a story to tell. Apparently, a group of believers first met in the home of one of Oliver Cromwell's Officers and by 1690 there were thirty-seven members. In 1721 this number had grown to fifty-six and the first Meeting House was built in Whitchurch. Over the years the membership fluctuated but the work of God continued and flourished. The Church moved to a new location in 1770 and still stands on the same site, having been refurbished and modernised in 2006. The membership of about twenty-five people welcomed Paul into their hearts and lives. They were so enthusiastic about having him with them and although they could not afford a full-time Minister, they helped him financially as much as they could. Paul encouraged them to start a weekly prayer meeting to seek God for the future of the Church. At times, it seemed that with no families or young people, the Church just would not be able to continue. However, over the period Paul was ministering there, the congregation grew and developed. God brought in a number of married couples with young children, which allowed the Church to think about re-starting the Sunday school and two very exciting and memorable occasions happened, when the Church celebrated their 360th Anniversary and when the Baptistery was opened for the first Baptism in ten years! God is so good.

When Paul finished his time at Whitchurch in July 2013, he was ordained as a Baptist Minister and Aylestone Baptist Church in Leicester called him to be their Minister. Whitchurch were able to appoint a young trainee minister to replace Paul and so the little Church with such a great history was able to continue its' witness.

What a journey God had brought Paul on! At this point, we are excited because we know that this is just the beginning of another chapter in the story of his life.

Chapter 16 – Claire

Claire admits that she cannot remember a time or a place when she asked Jesus into her life. Sometimes when you are brought up in a Christian family, it seems as though you have been a Christian all your life. Certainly, I felt the same and can remember different Church events when I would re-dedicate my life to Jesus. I would often say this prayer: 'Come into my heart Lord Jesus, shut the door and never go out again'. It is good to know that once you have invited Jesus into your life, He is not going to leave you, but as a child somehow I felt the need to keep asking! I often feel it is as though we invite Jesus into our house, and often push him into the cupboard under the stairs, possibly allowing Him out on occasions and especially on Sundays! He is longing to be allowed into every room of your house to clean it up and stay on show for everyone to see!

Apart from having a difficult time with colic when a baby, Claire also struggled with deafness as a young child. We did not realise until she had a hearing test at school that she was deaf in one ear and partially deaf in the other. Soon she was taken into Hospital to have her adenoids removed and grommets put in both ears to improve her hearing. In those days, parents were not allowed to stay overnight with their children and at five years old we had to leave her in the hands of the nursing staff, which was very hard for her and us! I remember, when she returned home and was riding her bike, she asked, "What is that strange ticking noise?" We had not realised that she had never heard the sound of the wheels going round!

Claire found school difficult. The three 'R's' did not come easy to her and she lacked confidence. So we encouraged her to learn to play the piano, recorder, clarinet and guitar and take up speech and drama lessons. Although she was always considered too shy to be given a part in a play at school, she was given opportunities at Church to take part in various plays and shows. She reached Grade Four piano, and entered many festivals and speech exams, gaining her Bronze, Silver and Gold medals in Guildhall, Speech and Drama. At eighteen years old she entered for the Teacher's Diploma, only missing by two marks. Possibly, she was considered to be too young, but sadly she never tried again. However, we shall see how God used these gifts and abilities in an incredible way as she progressed in her life.

As she grew up, Claire's social life revolved around the Church, going to Girls' Brigade and spending time with her friends from the Youth Group. She had one particular friend called Joanna, and they started a youth drama group and a junior orchestra. Both Claire and Joanna's drama and musical abilities were such a help to me as I led ninety, five to eleven year olds at Church! I could not have done it without them!

We never had any problems with Claire throughout the teenage years, apart from the fact that she loved to argue! Someone once said about their daughter, 'she thinks she knows everything, yet in reality knows nothing!' I am sure that sums up a lot of teenagers! No doubt you have seen the car sticker - 'hire a teenager whilst they know everything!'

Claire only had one rebellious time, which was whilst at College. For a week, she kept coming home early. One day saying the teacher had been shot in the eye, and another day the teacher had fallen down the stairs and broken her leg. The final reason was, there had been a fire at the college and everyone had been sent home! I am afraid I was so naive I believed her stories, until her Tutor rang me up to ask if Claire was ill, as she had not been to College for over a week!

At school, Claire studied a Child Care Course, which prepared her for going to St. Albans College where she trained for a diploma with the N.N.E.B. (Nursery Nurses Examination Board) Eventually, she started a job as a Nursery Nurse in a private kindergarten, teaching two to five year olds before they went to school, and she worked her way up to become Deputy Head.

Claire met John Greaves in the Church Youth Group. The first time I met John was when I found him asleep on our settee as I came downstairs to make breakfast! Little was I to know that within a few weeks he would be living with us and occupying our spare room for two years! John came from a Christian home, but before meeting Claire, he had been rebelling against God for a couple of years and had been thinking about going to America. As he did not have a job, he went to work with Martyn, helping in the Financial Services Company in St. Albans and eventually he went to work for the Ford Motor Company.

John and Claire were baptised at Luton Christian Fellowship, where eventually John became the Youth Leader. They were married on April 30th 1994 and went to live in Luton where their children, Nathan, Amy and Holly were born. We had the privilege of childminding Nathan from two months old, whilst Claire went back to work, and later we also looked after Amy. We really did feel those times were special and loved spending so much time with our grandchildren.

When Holly was three months old, the Greaves family sold their three-bedroom house and left to go and live in Cornwall. Claire and John believed God was leading them to start a retreat for Christians and help plant a Church. They met a Christian couple who used to go to their Church and now lived near Callington. Also they met a businessman who had a house with a large area of land, plus holiday cottages and he seemed to be keen to develop these. After much prayer, and consultation with others, they felt God was in this move and bought a holiday home.

Unfortunately, within a short space of time, everything seemed to go wrong. John was meant to be working with his friend as a builder, but the businessman decided to sell his existing house and land and bought a large house in need of refurbishing. He asked John's friend to do this work, but there was not enough work for the two of them, which left John without a job. So, there they were in the middle of the Cornish countryside in a very damp chalet, with their three small children and no money coming in. To make matters worse, during the winter they were completely flooded out, when a lane above them turned into a gushing river, and poured down the hill, in and around their home.

Life became more and more difficult and eventually nearly all their savings had gone; crying out to God had not appeared to help. They admit it was the lowest point of their lives - they were so sure that they had heard from God, yet everything had gone wrong.

Around this time, they met a woman who completely deceived them. Due to their circumstances, they were very vulnerable and she promised them so much in terms of worldly things. She supposedly was going to buy a restaurant and wanted them to help run it - although it turned out that the restaurant was not for sale! They picked out very expensive cars from a garage catalogue, which she was going to buy for them, but unfortunately they were never ordered. She took them to look round a million pound house which was for sale and promised she would buy this property for them to live in. That again did not happen. She talked about taking them abroad on holiday but that too never materialised. The lies were endless and eventually they realised it was all a terrible 'con-trick', even down to the fact that she produced a photocopy of her bank account, showing that she possessed a great deal of money - yet even that was a fake.

It was such a hard time for them, and they learned some very painful lessons. Looking back, we can see how the Devil was seeking to tempt and destroy at a time when they were struggling spiritually, emotionally, and financially.

Interestingly, King David in the Bible wrote some of his Psalms (songs) when he was experiencing deep despair and at his lowest ebb and Claire found that, as she cried out to God from deep within her, she too wrote some beautiful songs which later were put onto a CD. Sometimes in life, when we have been through the darkest valleys or the most barren deserts, we learn so much about our own fallibility and how much we really need God.

During this time, Martyn and I had moved to Paignton, Devon, and started going to an Assemblies of God (Pentecostal) Church. After a few weeks, Claire and John came to visit us, and accompanied us to Church. I remember a dear lady, called Margaret, who said, "They are such a lovely little family. We must pray for them to come and live here". I thought at the time, 'Why pray for that, they don't want to come and live here?' But God had other ideas!

In the weeks that followed, Claire and John travelled from Cornwall each Sunday. They often arrived in time for breakfast, then we all went to Church and they returned home after lunch. Not many people commute to Church! Eventually, they decided to sell up and come to live in Paignton. (Margaret's prayers were answered!) They rented a house and John had various jobs until he went to work for Torbay Council. Claire worked at a pre-school and for a year Martyn and I home-schooled Nathan and Amy, before they started at local schools.

After a while, through the generosity of my sister Valerie, who helped them with a deposit, they were able to buy their own house. They settled into the Church and John became the Youth Leader - a job which brought him much happiness and a number of headaches! Youth Leaders certainly need our prayers – and sometimes it is the parents of the young people who can cause the most problems! Claire joined the worship band and became a very gifted Worship Leader. She helped John with the Youth and started a Youth Band within the Church. God is so good. Often it is not until we look back and see what has happened in our lives that we realise how His hand has been upon us, leading and guiding, even if we have made some mistakes along the way. After a number of years they decided to take a much needed rest to see what God wanted them to do in the future.

As well as being a very busy working Mum with three children, Claire decided to study for a Foundation Degree in Early Years and Education, with a view to possibly using this in order to further her career at a later date. She also was able to use her musical skills and bring much joy to the elderly, by playing the piano and singing in the many Residential Care Homes in Torbay. Claire and John's story, and the journey of Nathan, Amy and Holly, obviously still continues and I am sure that one day another book will be written of their personal trials, and God's miraculous signs and wonders in their lives.

We have to keep reminding ourselves, that it is not our grandchildren who have experienced the wonderful things which God has done in our lives, therefore we must continually talk about them and record them for future generations to come. Our life stories are just an extension of those we read about in the Bible and we must never stop talking about what God is doing in the 21st Century.

Chapter 17 – Moving On

Perhaps you are wondering how Martyn and I ended up in Paignton, Devon?

We had not thought about moving from Harpenden, until one day in August 2002. My mother and oldest sister Valerie came to stay with us. We were sitting at our dining room table when the post arrived and there was an advertising leaflet saying - 'say no to the expansion of Luton Airport'. I remember having a conversation about the route of the new runway and how it could mean that the planes would take off and land over our house, and should that happen we would need to move. My sister said "Surely you would not move from here?" It was as if the seeds were being sown in our minds.

We began to see large signs everywhere regarding the expansion of the airport, and decided that perhaps we should think and pray about moving, but what about the childminding business and where should we go? Strangely enough, for the first time the business seemed to be rather quiet. Our babies had grown and were all at school and nobody asked if we had any vacancies. Then in October, Claire and John left Luton for Callington, Cornwall. People asked us, "Why don't you go and live in Cornwall?" However that did not feel right!

During the October half-term we went to visit Claire and John and decided to travel back via Torquay. We had spent a number of holidays there and loved the area. We knew Upton Vale Baptist Church in Torquay, due to the fact that we had slept on their floor with the young people from Stopsley, and on another visit we had stayed in the Assistant Minister's flat. So we wondered - if God brought us to Torquay, would we go to Upton Vale?

We spent the day looking at various houses which were for sale and we found a house with a granny flat attached. We knew that if we were to move we would need to take Martyn's parents with us. We had already uprooted them from Wakefield to Luton in 1990 because his Dad suffered with epileptic fits and they were dependent on us to look after them. In fact, we felt that, if they agreed to move, this would be 'our sign' that it was the right place to be. The house itself was a two hundred year old, refurbished coach house, with a huge open fireplace and big old oak beams. We had always admired similar houses shown in the television programmes *Midsomer Murders* or *Escape to the Country*! This was our dream house, with even a granny flat attached!

We went back home very excited and rushed to tell Martyn's parents all about it. When asked whether they would like to come with us, to our surprise they jumped at the opportunity. We put both our properties up for sale, and they sold within a week. It seemed as though God was opening all the doors. We packed everything into boxes, and then found that the gentleman who wanted to buy our house had lost his job and could not go ahead with the purchase after all. From that moment, we really struggled to sell our house. We were so sure that the granny flat was perfect for Martyn's parents. I could look after them and help when his Dad had epileptic fits; however, something happened to change all that!

In the February half-term of 2003 Claire and John travelled up from Cornwall to visit us in Harpenden. We were all in the park playing together; Claire was pushing Holly on the swing, Nathan was playing football with his Dad and Grandad, and I took four year old Amy to a part of the park where there were wooden bridges and climbing frames. Some logs were placed in a semi-circle (we now know they had been part of a large tree that had been cut down, and not removed by the contractors). Thinking that they were part of the park equipment I held Amy's hand whilst she walked on them. We played a game where she was escaping from the sharks! She said "Climb up here Nan, the sharks are coming". I duly stepped onto the logs and walked behind her. All of a sudden, one of the logs moved and my foot went down between the logs, and ended up pointing out at a quarter to nine position! I had a triple fracture and a dislocation of my left ankle! As I lay on the ground in excruciating pain, I told Amy to go and get Grandad. She ran off and shouted for everyone to come.

Whilst we waited for the ambulance, John held my foot in his hand and prayed in tongues. I remember, whilst he prayed it was like an anaesthetic; I felt no pain, but the minute he stopped praying the pain returned. When the paramedics arrived, they took me to the hospital where my ankle was pulled back into position. Anyone who has had a dislocation will know how painful that is! I was admitted to the ward and had an operation which involved inserting plates and screws into my ankle. Afterwards, the Consultant told me that there had been just about enough bone left to work with and to only expect, at the best, about seventy per cent movement back in my ankle.

During those first few weeks, I slept downstairs on the settee. My ankle became infected and the plaster was removed after a few days; however, the good news was that it enabled me to have lots of early physiotherapy treatment. I could only move around the house on my bottom and used a wheelchair when we went out. I was not sleeping well, and recall the night in March when Paul returned from the Discipleship Training Course in Cyprus, and we sat together into the early hours of the morning watching the start of the Iraq war. It is strange how one can remember certain important events so clearly - where you were, who you were with and what you were doing. It is like the night when President Kennedy was shot, or Princess Diana died in the car crash in France, or 9.11 when the planes crashed into the twin towers in New York. Somehow, these occasions are etched in one's mind for ever.

I had always imagined that if I ever became ill, I would use the time to read my Bible and Christian books. However, I found it difficult to concentrate, and even harder to pray! I knew God was with me throughout it all, and was aware of His presence, and that family and friends were praying for me. In fact, it brought home to me the importance of praying for those who are sick - sometimes people cannot pray for themselves and need others to do so. Neighbours said to me, "How can you remain so cheerful?" I can remember thinking that I just wanted to glorify God through it all. During trials is the time to put our faith into action - I did not know what the future held for me, but I trusted my Saviour was with me every step of the way.

By this time, the people who were buying Martyn's parents bungalow wanted to move in but there were no signs of our house being sold. We knew we could not proceed with the house we wanted to buy, so Martyn and I drove to Torquay and looked for somewhere for Martyn's parents to live. I became a connoisseur of the best disabled toilets at various service stations on the motorway! I also experienced how disadvantaged one feels in a wheelchair. Often people talk over you to the person pushing, and talk down to you as though you are mentally disabled, rather than have a physical problem!

McCarthy and Stone were in the process of building a block of new retirement flats in St. Marychurch, Babbacombe. They had only completed the downstairs flats but we signed up that day. In fact, Martyn's parents were the first people to move in whilst the builders were still working upstairs. I packed up all their possessions, and whilst Martyn drove them to Torquay, John hired a large van, and he and I followed behind with their furniture. By now, I was using crutches whilst hanging curtains, unpacking boxes, making beds and I thank God He gave me the strength and ability to do it all. The only problem was that we were still living in Hertfordshire (over four hours journey away) so every time

Martyn's Dad had an epileptic fit we had to rush off down to Torquay as his Mum could not cope on her own.

Eventually, after ten months we managed to sell our house in Harpenden. We found a bungalow in Broadsands, Paignton which we fell in love with, although it was a few miles across the Bay from Martyn's parents' flat. It was totally unsuitable for someone who was still walking with crutches (being situated on a hill and having steps to the front door and a hundred and fifty foot back garden with more steps!) However, as it turned out, it was the best physio treatment I could have had. I sat on my bike and free-wheeled down the hill to the sea, and used the bike as a zimmer frame to walk back home. For hours I walked in the sea with my crutches, pushing the waves back with my bad ankle. Within months I was walking and even running, and regained about ninety-five percent movement. The ankle is still sometimes painful and swollen but God is good. I may not be completely healed but I thank God I did not have to remain in that wheelchair.

Chapter 18 - The Journey Continues

Soon after we had moved to Paignton, Martyn and I were looking at the boats on the sea, and chatting about how God had blessed us so much by bringing us to such a beautiful part of the country, when Martyn said how it would be 'the icing on the cake' to be able to go out in a boat. A few days later, we were giving out leaflets outside the cinema to the people who had been to see the film, *The Passion of the Christ*. The Churches of Paignton had joined together to give out literature to provide further information about the death and resurrection of Jesus. Whilst we were standing outside the cinema, a young man in his twenties came up to Martyn and said, "Are you Martyn Wheeler?" He and his family had been part of our Church fellowship in Stopsley, and we had not seen him for about fifteen years! We had a good chat and found out that his auntie and uncle lived just down the road from where we lived. Later that day, his auntie called to see us and, to cut a long story short, we became good friends, and guess what? – she and her husband owned a beautiful three-bedroom, two-bathroom, luxury motor-boat, on which we had the privilege of spending many happy hours! God is so good.

Our first year in Paignton was quite difficult. We spent a lot of time looking after Martyn's parents. His Dad was very unwell and after only ten months in his flat, he fell and broke his hip and had to be looked after in a Nursing Home. Martyn's mother was very demanding and difficult and we had no idea how she would cope when his Dad eventually died (or how we would cope with her!) We could only pray and leave it to God. Ten days after he died, she fell and broke her hip and was unable to look after herself anymore. We found a really good Residential Care Home for her, where she settled and was quite content. We look back and realise why it had not worked out with that house with the Granny flat! God knows what the future holds and sometimes we wonder why our plans do not work out - yet He knows what is around the corner.

We had prayed for many years that Martyn's Mum would give her life to Jesus. Like so many people, she believed that she was a Christian and going to Heaven because she had been born and lived in a Christian country and was christened and confirmed into the Church of England. Whilst she was in the Care Home, Martyn and I took a small team of people into the Home once a month to sing hymns, share testimonies, read the Bible and pray with the elderly people. Many times she heard the good news about Jesus of how he died for her, to take away her sins and all she needed to do was to ask for forgiveness and give her life to Him and she would have eternal life. Only God knows whether she did accept Jesus as her Lord and Saviour - He alone knew what was in her heart.

In November 2011 she had a fall which resulted in her having to go into Hospital. She became very poorly and refused to eat or drink. It was a difficult time, watching her starve herself to death. Each day we were able to pray with her, for which she seemed grateful and one particular day I said the words of Psalm 23 and she mouthed the words of the first verse - 'The Lord is my Shepherd'. Just before Christmas, she was transferred back to the Residential Home. The day before she died, we led the annual Carol Service in the Home and my daughter Claire played the piano and Amy and Holly came to sing. After the service we all went into her room to sing 'Away in a Manger'. Somehow we all knew that this would be the last time we would see her alive and we were able to say our goodbyes. We thank God we had that special time with her and pray that one day we will all be reunited. Her funeral was particularly significant, as her grandson Paul led the service and gave a short sermon. It was the first funeral at which he had officiated and it must have been difficult emotionally; however, he was most professional and led it well. I could not help but think that she would have been so very proud of him.

When we first moved to Paignton, we attended an Assemblies of God Church. They believed in using the spiritual gifts, such as tongues, healing, prophecy and words of knowledge. The Pastor who originally started the Church was a man called Stan Hyde. He is in his eighties now, and I am sure in years to come a book will be written about the miracles God has done in and through him. He was just an ordinary man in the Navy, when God took hold of his life and started doing miraculous things through him. He planted a number of Churches in the South West of England, and he has diaries full of the incredible things that happened during his ministry, including someone being raised from the dead!

Over the six years at the Church, Martyn and I led Alpha Courses, Discipleship courses and headed up the Men's and Women's Ministries. I started an annual outreach event called 'Beautiful Inside and Out' - where we invited ladies in the local community to a free pamper evening. They were given free haircuts, manicures, makeovers, and massages for shoulders, hands and feet! There was a short talk to tell the ladies how they could also be beautiful on the inside by having a relationship with Jesus. It was great for people outside the Church to see that Christians were normal, and they went away having had a lovely evening, and wanting to come back again.

We were involved in a Church outreach event held on Paignton sea front. Martyn and I were in charge of the hospitality tent, and all was well until a tremendous wind blew the tent away. Within minutes the man involved with the 'donkey rides' came rushing up to Martyn blaming him for frightening his donkeys! Luckily, no damage was done and Martyn was able to smooth things over.

It reminded me of another time when a much bigger tent blew away. It was during our time at Luton Christian Fellowship, when all the local Churches worked together to bring the evangelist Luis Palau to speak at a large mission event. Much prayer and work had gone into the preparations, and everyone was very excited about the opportunity to invite friends and neighbours to such a big event. Sadly the weather on the day was dreadful, the Big Top was blown away, the field completely water-logged, and the evening had to be cancelled. Who knows why such a thing should happen? The one good thing which resulted from it was that the Churches were brought together and relationships were strengthened. During the week they were able to hold smaller meetings where Luis Palau spoke. Obviously it was not the large event that had been planned, but I know God used the smaller events in a completely different way. One such meeting was held in the Strathmore Hotel in Luton and Martyn was able to take his father to meet Luis Palau, which he would not have been able to do had the event been held in the Big Top. It is so good that God can take our trials and difficulties and use them to bring about His purposes if we trust in Him.

Sadly, it is a fact of life that, as we continue on our journey, we have to face saying goodbye to loved ones and friends as they leave this world. It always seems much harder when they leave us prematurely. My sister's husband John had been diagnosed with cancer and for some years he had been struggling with this horrible disease. He had walked with God since a boy and knew that he was going to spend eternity with Him, but it was still very hard for my sister and family to let him go. Everyone copes with grief in different ways and for them they decided to cover the coffin with pictures of John taken throughout his life, so that the coffin was literally a visual portrait of his journey here on earth.

We have a number of friends who are struggling with cancer and we long to see them healed, but as I have said before, we do not understand why some are healed and some are not. We can only trust God in all situations that His perfect will may be done. I had a very special friend who recently died of cancer. She shared with me that through her illness God had taught her so much, particularly about not judging people and how to love them unconditionally. When she was in the Hospice just a couple of weeks before she died, a friend and I took her to a service in the little Chapel there. Besides the Chaplain, we were the only people and it was a beautiful time. This dear lady chose all her favourite hymns and songs and then proceeded to share what God had done in her life. She was a shining example of how to cope with adversity and how to prepare to meet Jesus.

During our time in the Assemblies of God Church we were able to help people and made many good friends, but over a period of time, and with much thought and prayer, we felt it right to return to our Baptist roots and moved to Upton Vale Baptist Church in Torquay. I wonder whether God had wanted us there in the first place? It is sometimes hard to know exactly what God's will is but I have come to realise that even if we make mistakes, God can still use us, and bring us to where He wants us to be eventually. I feel sure God does not mind which denomination we are in, as long as we are receiving good sound Bible teaching, surrendering our lives to His will, and reaching out to those who do not know Jesus.

We had been asking God what He wanted us to do and how He wanted to use us, and the first week we were at Upton Vale, they announced that they would be starting debt counselling courses using an organisation called Christians Against Poverty. Martyn had already trained as a 'Money Coach' for this organisation, which provides free advice for people in debt. So he offered his help to run monthly courses at Upton Vale. We joined a housegroup, but after a year the group leaders moved on and we were asked to lead the group! We really felt God had answered our prayer and shown us exactly what He wanted us to do. We are excited about the future and look forward to how God will work out His purposes through us in the coming years.

Often when we say to God that we are prepared to be used in any way – look out, because we might be surprised at what happens! Certainly we were! Our nine year old grand-daughter Holly had been struggling to learn at school and we realised that she needed help. So we offered to home-school her for two years, in the hope that we could put her back into school after taking her eleven-plus exam. It was a huge commitment but so rewarding. It was a pleasure to see how she responded to one-to-one teaching and how grateful she was to have someone explain things to her. We felt it was a real privilege to have such an input into her young life, and not only help her with her education, but also teach her on a daily basis about the things of God - which we pray will stay with her all her life.

It was made all the more special to us when one day we shared with her how we felt that God had wanted us to home school her. She said "Do you mean that God loves and cares about me enough to bother about my education and whether I do well or not?" What a concept to have grasped at nine years old - that God loves her so much and cares about every detail of her life and is bothered about her future. Many people spend a lifetime without realising how much God loves and cares for them.

Chapter 19 – Walking with God

This has been the story of one family, and some of the people we met during our journey. We know the world has changed in so many ways since we were born; however, the great news is that God never changes. He is the same, yesterday, today and forever. I see our lives as being rather like a jig-saw, with pieces being added one at a time. Some have been difficult and some easy, but eventually they will all come together and we will see the big picture that God planned for us.

As we look at the first Book of the Bible, Genesis, we see the story of one family. It tells of the good and bad things that happened to them and how God worked in their lives, to bring them where he wanted them to be. If you think your family life is complicated, take a look at their lives! Although they went through tremendous difficulties, God was with them - even when they were not aware of it. That is exactly my experience of life, even at my lowest periods (and there have been some!) I can honestly say now, looking back, I know God has been right there supporting and carrying me throughout the journey.

I love the verses in Genesis 5:21-24 that tell us that -

'Enoch walked with God; then he was no more!' One version of the Bible says - *'Enoch walked in habitual fellowship with God.'*

How wonderful that Enoch and God experienced three hundred years of chatting and delighting with each other. Then one day, God just said "Come on home with me today". What a wonderful way to go! The Hebrew word 'charbar' means coupled together or in close fellowship. When I was at school, I remember having one best friend and we would walk around the playground arm in arm - no-one could separate us, we were coupled together. How great to be coupled together with God!

Jude:14-15 tell us that Enoch cried out against ungodliness and immorality, by warning people of God's coming judgement to punish men and women for their ungodly deeds. Hebrews 11:5 says that Enoch pleased God. What an epitaph!

I look back over my life and wonder why God seemed so active and ready to do miracles at certain periods more than others. Was it that I was more receptive to the Holy Spirit's power at work? Possibly, or is it that God's Holy Spirit works at certain times in our lives for certain purposes, as He wills? It is interesting that some Christians of 'our age' speak of a 'real move of God' back in the 1980's and 1990's and how they experienced God working in their Churches and lives in a special way.

In the Bible, we see that there were four hundred years of what appears to be God's silence, between the last Book of the Old Testament, Malachi, and the first Book of the New Testament, the Gospel of Matthew. Then he used one man, John the Baptist, to prepare the people spiritually for the coming of Jesus. Could it be, during those years of silence, God was still at work in people's lives but perhaps nobody recorded it?

This made me determined to write down the trials, signs and wonders that have accompanied our lives, so in years to come people will not just say miracles happened in the Bible. They do happen today. The stories in this book are proof of that and we need to be open to God's Holy Spirit to allow Him to work in us and through us, and have His way in our lives.

I have spent hours compiling our family history, looking back at our ancestors, in the many different censuses - when and where they were born, married and died. What was their occupation, and who were their children? It struck me, that there contained on a page is a person's entire life! Most of them I know little about. However, I do know that my mother's family originated from Devon and that my grandparents were Christians, grew up in Paignton and were Sunday School teachers at Paignton Baptist Church. My grandfather went on to be a Sunday School Superintendent at a Church in Uxbridge, Middlesex. I discovered that my great grandfather's brother was a Sunday School Teacher and a Deacon in the Congregational Church in Kingskerswell, just up the road from Paignton! In the 1920's two other members of the family left Devon to settle in Canada where they became Methodist Ministers. Although much of my life has been spent in different parts of England, as I now walk through the streets of Paignton, I find it strange to think that I am following in the steps of my family who lived here over a hundred years ago.

The Bible talks about us living for three score years and ten, so if we live longer than seventy years, as many of us do nowadays, it is as though we are on borrowed time! As I am fast approaching that 'famous age' it causes me to wonder and think about my life. In years to come, will my descendants just see me as a name and a life restricted to a page? What have I done with my life, and what am I still doing for God? Am I retiring or re-firing?

The Bible says – *'Therefore we do not lose heart. Though outwardly we are wasting away, yet inwardly we are being renewed day by day.'* (2 Corinthians 4:16)

It was not until I was older that I realised that my grandparents had constantly prayed for my sisters and myself and that our lives are products of their prayers. May I encourage you to realise the importance of covering your children and grandchildren in prayer. Paul, in the Bible, refers to the sincere faith of a young man called Timothy who was taught by his mother and grandmother from an early age. We need to constantly pray and talk to our children of what God has done and is still doing.

I am aware that my grandchildren all enjoy singing, playing the piano and performing! They perhaps do not realise that their musical gifts have been passed down through the generations. As well as both their parents being gifted in their musical and dramatic abilities, they inherit a rich musical and dramatic background! My grandmother taught my mother to play the piano when she was a young girl, and she became an accomplished pianist, singer and actress! My sisters and I were all encouraged to play the piano and sing and both Martyn and I were involved in performing on the stage. Martyn's father sang in the Church choir as a small boy, played the tenor horn in the Army Band and loved all kinds of music. Despite this wonderful heritage of music and drama, my greatest prayer is that personal faith in the Lord Jesus Christ, which has spanned the generations of our family, will continue in the lives of my grandchildren and their descendants and that they will be committed to walk with God.

I often wonder what my grandchildren will do with their lives and what experiences with God they will have along the way. I pray that they will be like Enoch and 'please God'.

There is a verse in John 21:25 which says -

'Jesus did many other things as well. If every one of them were written down, I suppose that even the whole world would not have room for the books that would be written.'

Other verses, in John 20:30-31, say -

'Jesus did many other miraculous signs in the presence of His disciples, which were not recorded in this book. But these are written that you may believe that Jesus is the Christ, the Son of God, and that by believing you may have life in His name.'

That is why I felt compelled to write this book. My prayer is that by seeing how God has worked in our family life and reading about some of the miracles He performed, you will believe that Jesus Christ is the Son of God. Also, that you will be encouraged to ask Jesus to take control of your life and fill you with His Holy Spirit. May your life be transformed and may you have complete assurance that you will spend eternal life with Him.

I will finish this book with words from Daniel 4:2-3 which sum up everything I have tried to say -

'It is my pleasure to tell you about the miraculous signs and wonders that the Most High God has performed for me. How great are His signs, how mighty His wonders! His Kingdom is an eternal Kingdom; His dominion endures from generation to generation.'